LIFE ON PLANET EARTH

User's Guide

LIFE ON PLANET EARTH
User's Guide

CECIL JENKINS

Copyright © 2024 Cecil Jenkins

The moral right of the author has been asserted.

Apart from any fair dealing for the purposes of research or private study, or criticism or review, as permitted under the Copyright, Designs and Patents Act 1988, this publication may only be reproduced, stored or transmitted, in any form or by any means, with the prior permission in writing of the publishers, or in the case of reprographic reproduction in accordance with the terms of licences issued by the Copyright Licensing Agency. Enquiries concerning reproduction outside those terms should be sent to the publishers.

Troubador Publishing Ltd
Unit E2 Airfield Business Park
Harrison Road, Market Harborough
Leicestershire LE16 7UL
Tel: 0116 279 2299
Email: books@troubador.co.uk
Web: www.troubador.co.uk

ISBN 978 1 83628 009 5

British Library Cataloguing in Publication Data.
A catalogue record for this book is available from the British Library.

Printed and bound in Great Britain by 4edge Limited
Typeset in 11pt Adobe Garamond Pro by Troubador Publishing Ltd, Leicester, UK

For Maeve, Max, William, Rosie, Charlie and Patrick
Late Millennials / Generation Z

CONTENTS

1. WELCOME TO YOUR WORLD — 1
   Life on planet earth
2. WHAT MAKES YOU YOU — 14
   Nature or Nurture?
3. THE YOU IN THE MIRROR — 23
   Male or female
4. YOUR PHYSICAL INHERITANCE — 34
   Luck of the draw
5. FAMILIES — 48
   And everybody has one
6. FAMILY DYNAMICS — 58
   Don't get mangled in the machine
7. BIRTH ORDER — 66
   Do you fit the stereotype?
8. WEALTH AND SOCIAL CLASS — 76
   Where are you on the ladder?
9. LIVING IN HISTORY — 86
   Social and political change

10. VALUES AND BELIEFS Religions and ideologies	94
11. RELATIONSHIPS Social and romantic	103
12. FACING THE FUTURE Climate change and its consequences	112
13. FACING THE FUTURE AI and darker matters	122
14. LIVING IN TIME Lifespan, ageing and death	132

1. WELCOME TO YOUR WORLD
Life on planet earth

Congratulations, you're the One.

And you're not just one in a million, you're one in a million million!

Aldous Huxley, the guy who wrote *Brave New World*, put it in a nutshell, or at least in an indifferent poem:

> A million million spermatozoa,
> All of them alive,
> Out of that cataclysm but one poor Noah
> Dare hope to survive,
> And among that billion minus one
> Might have chanced to be
> Shakespeare, another Newton, a new Donne –
> But the One was me.

So you're the One. You've beaten the enormous odds against you. You've won the gigantic lottery of existence. You're here. You've made it.

Mmm...?
Of course you might spare a thought for the other million million minus one spermatozoa who didn't make it, who weren't such strong swimmers, who didn't propel themselves with their tails powerfully enough, who go back into oblivion as sad little ghosts of nameless might-have-beens who will never get another chance. But life is a competitive business, so you can't afford to linger on it. Even less should you linger on the far larger fact that you emerged from only one of countless erotic episodes going on at the same time, so that there are a million million times your million million spermatozoa friends on the go at any one moment. If you try to calculate the odds you'll find the mathematics terrifying, it will give you vertigo, it could lead to madness – or even to the conclusion that you're just some sort of accident. But you're not, are you? The mathematics simply prove that you've beaten fantastic competition, that you've won the cosmic lottery – that you're the One. Any questions?

I don't know yet, I've just got here.
It'll be all right so long as you remember: you're the One.

So that means I'm the only One?
Well, not quite. There are other special Ones around, just like you. Quite a few of them in fact – around eight billion of them, and rapidly increasing at the last count.

Isn't that an awful lot?
Not really when you look at the mathematics. And remember that they have all beaten near-impossible odds, just like you. You're *all* special Ones, all eight billion of you.

1. WELCOME TO YOUR WORLD — Life on planet earth

So where on earth are we?
On earth, actually, now that you mention it. And congratulations again: you've hit the only spot where we know that life exists – on the cooled crust of a burning hot ball that we call a planet.

That doesn't sound too nice.
Well it's nicer than a planet like Kepler 438b, in the constellation of Lyra, which is rockier and hotter and for all we know could host horrors that we wouldn't even want to dream of. Fortunately, it's 470 light years away, so we won't have to worry about it for the next ten thousand years or so – though we might have to worry about the planet Wolf 1061c, which is 14 light years away.

That sounds kind of close.
Yes, it's barely more than 75 trillion miles. Meanwhile, we're lucky to be living on a planet that's nicely tucked away between a few other planets with godlike names like Mars and Venus and Neptune that revolve around a much bigger burning hot ball 93 million miles away from us that we call the sun.

Isn't 93 million miles another big number?
Not really, when you consider that Neptune is around 2.7 billion miles away, that our star the sun is only one star in a huge galaxy of stars, that it is a billion times smaller than a star like VY Canis Majoris, or that our galaxy is far smaller than a galaxy like IC 1011 which is 350 million light years away. Or, indeed, that our whole universe of galaxies may

| 3

be part of an unending multiverse or multiverses, and that if you looked through the new James Webb space telescope at the galaxy UDF 423, which is around 10 billion light years away, you would be looking – or trying to look, since it might no longer be there at all – billions of years into the past.

The past?
Ah yes: time. I was forgetting about time. So let's just mention in passing that our own solar system was formed sometime around 4.5 billion years ago – from the dust and debris left after the collapse of a giant molecular cloud.

But that's terrifying! You're telling me that we're stuck on a tiny speck of a burning hot ball that's rolling around in the middle of nowhere?! Can I go back where I came from?
That's not possible, I'm afraid! OK, so it's true, as this guy called Carl Sagan points out, that we ourselves are made of starstuff and that everyone and everything we have ever known exists on this tiny little speck – but doesn't that just show how lucky you are, in beating enormous odds time after time? Of course, I'm not saying that there aren't slight inconveniences from time to time…

What 'inconveniences?!
Oh you know, things like the Covid-19 pandemic, global warming, tsunamis, avalanches, volcanoes, earthquakes and the odd dirty great rocky meteor slamming into you from outer space – not to mention black holes.

1. WELCOME TO YOUR WORLD — Life on planet earth

What's a black hole?
Oh that's just a spot where the multiverse is eating itself.

Eating itself?!
Turning itself inside out might be a better way of putting it – a cosmic recycling centre.

But we're not in a black hole at the moment, are we?
I don't think so – at least nobody has mentioned it. But you've got to keep looking on the bright side.

What 'bright side'?!
Well, if an enormous meteor hadn't slammed into earth 65 million years ago and killed off these lolloping big creatures called dinosaurs, there would have been no room or reason for us to appear on the scene. Anyway, our own little corner of the cosmos is relatively cosy, with the sun to warm us in the daytime and a moon – which is a mere 240 thousand miles away after all – to shine upon us at night. And above all, for all we know, we may have the distinction and the dignity of being the most important feature of the multiverse.

How?
Our consciousness may be the only way the multiverse is aware that it exists – or not, of course.

OK, so everything lasts for millions of years. And I'll last millions of years as well?
Ah well, not quite, you'll be lucky to make eighty. But then, that's one of the things that make you special.

What is?
That you're the only living creature that knows it's going to die.

What's good about knowing you're going to die?
It gives you perspective, sharpens your thinking.

It's getting sharper by the minute! So, after all that, what exactly am I?
Well, there's good news and there's bad news – and they come in the same package.

I could do with some good news!
Well, the good news – and you deserve congratulations yet again – is that you have been born into the most highly developed of all the species there have ever been on earth: the humans who represent the highest form of life that anybody knows of, the very summit of evolution.

Evolution?
Ah yes, well, I'll try to explain. We're primates, you see, but we've changed a lot from just being apes or monkeys swinging around trees and making funny noises in the forest…

You mean I used to be a monkey?! This is ridiculous!
Well, a lot of people found it ridiculous when this poor devil Charles Darwin suggested it. He was so worried about it himself that he suffered from ulcers, migraines, dyspepsia, narcolepsy, flatulence, constipation, boils and depression,

not to mention the disapproval of his wife, who probably agreed with the upright churchmen that he had brought it all upon himself with his shameful, sinful ideas. But we split off from other primates, you see, started making stone tools two and a half million years ago, learnt to cook around four hundred thousand years ago and began to write five thousand years ago. We've come a long way since we switched to walking on two legs six million years ago. Hard to believe, isn't it?

You can say that again!
So now we're top of the tree. We domesticate other animals, we train them to work for us, we farm them and eat them, we put them in zoos when they're a bit unusual, we use them for medical experiments and – just so long as they don't look too unlike us – we turn them into pets. We are the master race around here. So that's pretty good, isn't it?

Well, if that's the good news, I hardly dare to ask you about the bad news.
That's part of the good news: that we have developed far bigger brains than the others.

So how is it bad news?
Well, if you're born a calf or a foal in a field, you can stagger to your feet, look around a bit, start feeding and, since your little brain doesn't have to bother to learn to talk or to ponder philosophical questions, you can almost immediately become independent. But with your bigger brain, you're completely dependent.

Isn't that sort of illogical?
That's just the way humans have evolved, you see. So when you arrive you can't even cling to your mother like a monkey or a chimpanzee, let alone move around. And of course you can't walk or talk yet since you've no words to talk with and therefore nothing to say. It's the price you pay for your superiority.

I believe you!
Yes, it's because your brain still goes on developing after birth and it's a couple of years before you can say simple things or even recognise yourself in the mirror. So with the logic and language parts of your brain developing so slowly, you've no words or concepts or idea of causation with which to form a sense of what's going on around you. Which is a bit of a downside perhaps.

Another one?
Well it can lead you to over-invest in the Unconscious, as that old Austrian guru Sigmund Freud would put it. You're in a kind of cave of dreams and nightmares, a place without reasons, a world of inexplicable delights and terrors, holiness and evil, gods and devils, ghosts and vampires.

Sounds awful!
Yes, but most people grow out of all that these days. Sort of, since you still get the odd individual who still believes in the Devil and choirs of angels, while late-night TV programmes and computer games can satisfy any lingering atavistic need to give yourself a little scare with staring-

eyed aliens, zombies, mysterious knockings on the ceiling or whatever.

So how can a baby cope with all this?
Well, it's not as bad as it sounds because, as this other guy Donald Winnicott pointed out years ago, there's no such thing as a baby.

This gets worse and worse.
No, he was saying that the baby isn't alone, that you have to think in terms of baby-and-mother. Because there's a symbiotic relationship between you and her.

Symbiotic?
Yes, you're inter-dependent. The baby comes out of the mother and feeds from the mother's body, so she's designed to feel as attached to the baby as the baby to the mother.

So she's special as well?
Well giving birth is a bit mysterious after all, she probably thinks you're a little miracle and, since she sees you as her achievement, she is conditioned to want and need to complete the task of bringing you up and being proud of you. And that's where you begin to get into the game.

The game?
Yes, inter-dependence is necessarily a balancing act, a game that you learn to play. At first, of course, she's only a dark blob like everything else, but she's the big warm soft blob that you feed from, the blob that seems to respond when you cry, the

blob that strokes and comforts you when you're distressed. But gradually, and the more intimately because you've no words to express yourself with, it becomes a little lover's game in which you smile when she smiles, you laugh when she laughs or get upset when you feel that she is upset. It's through that interdependence that you begin to acquire some power.

Power?
Yes, all games, nice or not, are ultimately about power. You learn how to cry and make your mother come to you, you learn how to please and you learn how to tease. You learn how to crawl around the room, tear books out of bookcases and display your cheeky little skills to make your mum and dad think you're wonderful. You discover that those big figures around you are easy to please. And that enables you to throw your weight around.

So how do I throw my weight around?
By throwing your sloppy, messy food around for a start. And then by practising the old highchair trick.

So what's that?
They've put you in your highchair at mealtime. You've finished eating that mushy glug stuff they feed you and your mum looks pleased with you. You smile and drop the spoon on the floor. She almost unthinkingly picks it up. You smile, then drop it again. Your dad picks it up this time. You smile and drop it a third time. They laugh at the realization that you are doing it deliberately, look at you admiringly and hand it to you again. They expect you to drop it again, as though to continue

the game, but you don't, so they go back to talking. At which point you drop the spoon again, causing them to look at you sharply as though wondering whether this might be a different game. Your dad hands you the spoon again and they wait for you to throw it down. So you wait, look at them levelly, smile – and don't throw the spoon down. At which point you see a flicker of doubt in their eyes as it dawns on them. That you're in charge. For it's actually quite routine, you see. Babies have been training and domesticating their mums and dads for aeons.

So who is this dad character you're talking about?
Oh yes, I should have mentioned that! There are these two main genders, you see: women like your mum and men like your dad.

Why?
That's a deep question, but they're sort of complementary. And it takes one of each to make a baby.

How?
They go into a sort of clinch and pant and yell a bit.

Does it hurt?
Not normally, in fact it can be very nice. It's called sex. Not that everybody does it – indeed starfish, sea anemones, flatworms, ants and whatnot can reproduce on their own.

Why?
They're less sophisticated and it saves time and energy, I suppose.

So sex is better?
Yes, it brings more variety into the species and it's generally more fun. As it obviously needs to be.

Why?
Well if it wasn't fun people might stop doing it and we'd all be dead. So it's built in as a drive or a necessity. As that fine feminist French philosopher Simone de Beauvoir put it – admittedly a little stiffly – sex is the assertion of the species against the individual.

So she didn't do it then?
What do you mean 'she didn't do it?'! Of course she did it! She was perfectly entitled to do it – and swing both ways in doing it! Why on earth do people think, just because she's an existentialist philosopher, that she didn't do it?! Of course she did it…!

Sorry, I didn't realise I'd touched a nerve.
No no, my fault. It's sometimes just a little stressful explaining what we're doing on the cooled crust of a burning hot ball in the middle of a gigantic Nowhere…

I thought maybe that you and she…?
No no, she died long ago. Actually, it may be the name that gets me. She's a fine feminist writer of course, but she's got such a wonderful romantic aristocratic name: Si-mone de Beau-voir, Si-mone de Beau-voir… Can't you feel it?

No.
Oh well, it'll come. So where were we?

1. WELCOME TO YOUR WORLD — Life on planet earth

On the cooled crust of a burning hot ball in the middle of a gigantic Nowhere.
No no! I mean what were we talking about – *before* Simone de Beauvoir?

Sex?
Ah yes, sex. But of course, as Simone would have pointed out, sex isn't quite the same as gender.

More complications?
I'm afraid so. But it's a bit of a minefield, so we had better tread carefully. It's all about Nature or Nurture.

2. WHAT MAKES YOU YOU

Nature or Nurture?

OK, so there are men and women, didn't we say? And at least people agree that there are basic physiological differences between them, so you can normally tell the ones from the others. For a start, men are generally taller and more muscular, which guaranteed their ability to run around the forest chasing wild animals in the old days, while they also developed deeper voices and hairy chests and beards.

Why?
To signal that they were mature and ready for action with the ladies. Who of course have different internal organs for producing babies, breasts for feeding them, a bigger thyroid, a quicker heartbeat and a smaller lung capacity. Oh, and they live longer than men.

Because they weren't running around the forest chasing wild animals?
That might have been a factor, plus the fact that men often die in battle or industrial accidents or because they have generally

smoked more – though women are beginning to catch up. Incidentally, the first finger of a woman's hand tends to be longer than the third, while with men it's the opposite.

What's that about?
I've no idea, unless it was to enable your hairy-chested guy in the forest to give his rivals the finger. But it goes to show at least that men and women are different.

So what's the problem?
Well, the first problem is that when it comes to sex and mating, the difference isn't as clear or as absolute as you might expect. Sexual identity, as old man Freud pointed out, exists over a wide spectrum. But though there are lots of special cases, a US national survey of sexual inclinations found five different categories.

Still sounds like a lot.
Of course, over 90% of both men and women were heterosexual – or straight, as we say.

And the rest were bent?
No, we call it gay. So 8% of men declared themselves to be gay, with 7% of women saying similarly that they were Lesbian, though there were also around 3% of men and 4% of women who said they were bisexual – if only on weekends.

It's all a bit complicated, isn't it?
Yes, it is, especially since some people strayed experimentally on occasion into another group – especially if they were in

a prison or a monastery or boarding school or some other single-sex set-up. But that still doesn't take account of another group, the transsexuals.

Who are they then?
Well they're people who think there has been a mistake somewhere in the process of being conceived and born, men who feel they're really women and women who feel they're really men in the wrong skin.

That sounds like a bum deal.
You could put it that way. And it often causes them so much embarrassment and suffering that they get a surgical operation to get themselves turned around.

Sounds awful! And you still haven't got to your fifth category, have you?
I'm getting there! They're the asexuals, the 1% of people who have no sexual inclination.

They just find it a pain in the ass?
They don't even get that far. They apparently just find it a pointless, sweaty, sticky business, and think the whole thing is a bit of a bore. As compared with stamp collecting, I suppose, or playing computer games, or having a nice chat with crumpets over afternoon tea.

I don't know! This whole gender business sounds a ridiculously confused system.
Yeah well, it takes all sorts! Though not everybody would

agree. There are straight people who think it's wrong and even sinful to be gay, that you should pull yourself together or pray and just stop being gay. There are places on the planet where they kill you for being gay – just to teach you not to be gay.

Can you stop being gay?
Well, around forty years ago even gay people tended to say that being gay was a 'sexual preference', almost as you might have a preference for jam sponge over strawberry ice cream. But nobody takes that very seriously these days. If you're gay you're gay. But that's leading us into this great argy-bargy over Nature or Nurture. And I don't have to tell you where those terms come from.

Simone de Beauvoir?
No no, William Shakespeare.

Who's he?
He's that famous dramatist who was around four hundred years ago – and for somebody so well-known he's really quite good.

He'd be pleased to hear it!
He opposes nature and nurture in this play called *The Tempest*, but of course the question itself was asked as far back as the ancient Greeks, and the argument really hotted up a hundred and fifty years ago after the emergence of the idea of evolution. Are you the way you are because of what you inherited, that's to say Nature, or because of the

influence of your family and society after you're born, that is to say Nurture?

Sounds like a good question.
Especially since it had all sorts of social and political implications – on both sides of the argument. Darwin's second cousin Francis Galton, who batted for the Nature side, thought that intelligence was inherited and wanted to improve society through 'better breeding', which encouraged some very controversial ideas.

Which were?
That some races are inherently inferior and that the deformed and the mentally ill should be prevented from reproducing themselves. The American Eugenics Society argued for that a century ago and of course it was actually carried out in Nazi Germany under Adolf Hitler, who declared himself to be the leader of a blond handsome Aryan master race.

Well, if he was blond and handsome himself, I suppose…
But he wasn't, now that you mention it. He was dark with a squashed nose, his propaganda chief Goebbels was tiny with a club foot, his air force boss Goering was a drug addict the size of an airship, his SS chief Himmler couldn't see as far as his feet – and that's only the leaders of the outfit!

Sounds like they were over-compensating.
Over-compensating to the point of murdering millions of Jews, Slavs, gays and trade unionists among others. All of which helped to shift the pendulum towards the Nurture

side of the argument. To people who believed that when you come into the world you're just a 'tabula rasa'.

Sounds painful! What's that?
A 'blank slate' on which your family and social environment then inscribe your character, for good or ill. This behaviourist chap John B. Watson claimed he could take any child at random and, no matter what his inherited characteristics were, turn him into whatever he fancied: a lawyer, an artist, a thief, or a roadside bum.

And did he?
Not really, though he did change the conditioned responses of the odd rat or rabbit – and made it big in advertising. And this whole environmental Nurture approach got very important with the growth of the social sciences in the last century. For reasons that I need hardly spell out.

So why do I feel somehow that you're going to?
Oh well, if you push me. OK, so the whole argument obviously had ideological, moral and political implications. If you take the Nature side of the argument and argue, as some did, that black people have a lower IQ than white – while ignoring different levels of wealth, education and other environmental factors – you are setting the scene for unequal treatment of minorities. And people didn't like that.

I can see why.
Similarly, if you argue that women are less intelligent and

competent than men, you are preparing the way for them to be held back in politics, work and the home.

And they didn't like that either?
Precisely. And of course, that's part of the reason why it could be said that it takes a long time to become a woman – I need hardly tell you by whom.

William Shakespeare?
No no, Simone de Beauvoir! And that's not all that they didn't like about the Nature side of the argument. For if you believe that somebody goes around murdering people because he has inherited the wrong genes and can't help it, the poor devil, that raises the question of whether he can be considered responsible for his actions or judged to be guilty. And nobody could accept that.

So the Nurture side won the argument?
Not really. Because they overplayed their hand by denying that there could be any significant differences whatever between races or men and women, and by saying there was no hereditary influence when studies of twins, for example, demonstrated that there was.

Then which side did win the argument, Nature or Nurture?
Neither. In fact, the question was considered naïve. For one thing, it was obvious that there were *both* hereditary and environmental influences on all of us. And, for another, these were often so difficult to disentangle because they were interdependent – as with eye colour, for example. You inherit the

colour through your parents, but the environment is still a factor since the colour – whether it is light blue in Sweden or dark brown in equatorial Somalia, say – would also have been affected originally by the intensity of the sunlight in a particular latitude.

So where are we now?
Well, we now have this ambitious Human Genome Project, which has identified genes for diseases such as cystic fibrosis or breast cancer, and which holds out hope for the analysis and treatment of the ageing disease Alzheimer's among others. It is leading to a revolution in biotechnology, and it should illuminate how we evolved and separated from other primates – not to mention the genetic similarities between ourselves. It is already playing an important role in genetic modification of plants such as wheat, to produce disease-resistant and more productive crops for a famine-threatened world.

That sounds great!
Yes, but all this, instead of providing the nice, neat answers some people were expecting, has revealed the extraordinary complexity of the whole issue. For it shows, as our big-bearded friend Dan Dennett sees it, that the mind is a product not just of natural selection but of cultural redesign of enormous importance.

And is Dan Dennett's big beard a product of cultural redesign?
What?! You're not being cheeky, are you?

No no...
It's just that he's a philosopher, with a striking beard, for heaven's sake! Anyway, the point is that it is not so much Nature *or* Nurture as Nature *via* Nurture, since the hereditary element is conditioned by the particular environment, set of circumstances and life history of each individual – which of course are unique to each of us. Everybody is different. Which goes to show, as I was trying to tell you...

That I'm special?
Precisely. That you're special. So special we can now treat you as a teenager faced with the problems people experience every day.

But am I male special or female special?
We're just coming on to that, so you can decide for yourself.

---

3. THE YOU IN THE MIRROR
Male or female
___

OK, so let's assume you look identifiably human, and that you don't suffer from any birth defect or disfigurement as some unlucky people do, so what's the first thing you notice when you look in the mirror?

That I exist?
And that you're male or female, I suppose. Some of the differences are physiological, such as the basic shape of the body, the genitalia and the presence or absence of breasts. Some are merely conventional and therefore optional, such as long hair, face make-up or more colourful clothes for women, or shaved heads or beards like Dan Dennett's for men, but these fashions change and people increasingly have different ways of presenting themselves as masculine or feminine, or something in-between.

More fuzziness?
Yes, but there are broad differences in all sorts of ways.

For example, girls are physically and neurologically more advanced at birth, while boys are more vulnerable to disease and hereditary defects. And girls have better verbal skills, while boys have better visual and spatial skills.

So there are real differences then?
Yes, but it's not quite so simple. For one thing, there's a lot of overlap between boys and girls in relation to these skills and, for another, the differences also respond to the different situation in which men and women find themselves. It may be true that a man's testosterone makes him more aggressive, while a woman's inability to produce as much serotonin makes her worry more, but then she might be better at seeing what there is to worry about – and that's where evolution and culture come in, isn't it?

Is it?
Yes, for example if men tend to have more spatial awareness, it might be because they needed it for hunting, while if women are better at distinguishing colours and smells, it might be because they needed to be able to distinguish poisonous plants or rotten food when they were lumbered with the cooking. And if men are more interested in things and women in personal relationships, it doubtless connects with women's historic role as mothers and carers. But the situation is changing now that we're in an age of transition.

An age of transition?
Since we live in time, God help us, we're always in an age of transition, whether we like it or not!

3. THE YOU IN THE MIRROR — Male or female

God...?
Oh, that's something else, we'll talk about all that later. I was just making the point that the situation has been changing over the past fifty years since the arrival of the Pill.

The Pill?
Yes, the Pill. Until this convenient form of contraception became available, women had no real control over their own fertility. They could have baby after baby and spend their best years looking after them, with no financial or legal independence and no freedom to work or engage actively in the society they lived in – as still happens in poor countries. But now, at least in this society, they can get jobs and indeed, since they tend to be better equipped than men for the post-industrial economy, they can often earn more. So they're sort of equal.

'Sort of' equal...?
Yes, because there is something of a hangover from the old days, a lot of lingering confusion over sex and gender – gender being rather the identity conferred upon men and women by the differing roles in society. And there are a couple of reasons for this, the first being simply that it takes time for attitudes to change. Children as they grow up tend obviously to conform to what they are supposed to be like as boys or girls, and these gender identities are reinforced in all innocence by the attitudes of their parents and their teachers, not to mention the stereotypes promoted by children's books, the cinema and television. And so, to take a colourful example, you get the old pink-or-blue preference.

What's that?
Go into a shop selling baby clothes and you can still find a pink section with frilly clothes for girls and a blue section with manly gear for boys. This despite the fact that children under the age of two have been shown to demonstrate no colour preference and that a hundred years ago the fashion was the direct opposite: pink for boys and blue for girls. This does not prevent an arms manufacturer in the United States today from producing pretty little pink rifles for pretty little girls in pink dresses to shoot their pretty little friends with.

Sounds pretty awful.
You could say that! Similarly, it has been shown that there is no innate gender preference as between dolls or toy cars before the age of twelve months, when the conditioning cultural effect kicks in. Which brings us to power.

Power...?
Yes, the other reason why there is confusion over sex and gender is a change in the power relationship between men and women. People have lived for thousands of years in patriarchal societies with a male god, a male ruler, male priests, male heroes, male landowners, male factory owners, male lawyers and even male doctors to treat women – sometimes mutilating them to prevent them from experiencing sexual pleasure, sometimes idealising them as pure virgins or mother figures as a subtle way of seeing them as non-sexual and keeping them subservient. Women had no place in the big bad world, they belonged to the private domain, they had to be controlled, so that they would

support their husband and, to a large extent, do what they were told.

It was a man's world?
Yes, but it wasn't simply the fault of the men. It was due essentially to the fact that women were chained to the home because of their inescapable child rearing and housekeeping duties, which prevented them from taking part in civic or political affairs. This, of course, was assumed to be the natural and therefore permanent order of things, embodied in the marriage vow whereby the bride promised to obey the husband – after being 'given away' by her father. This was the glue with which they held the old social structure together – or tried to.

It didn't always work?
It worked fairly well at one level, since they could keep the peace between families and even countries by offering a daughter in marriage to a potential rival. Indeed, this trading of princesses as a form of diplomatic exchange became a way of trying to keep the peace in Europe – though it often broke down, as when the Tsar Nicholas II of Russia and King George V of Great Britain lined up against their cousin the Emperor Wilhelm II of Germany in the First World War. But at home, of course, there was another problem to manage, the potentially disruptive effect of you-know-what.

Do I?
Well, you ought to by now.

Is it sex?
Good, you're coming along. Yes, sex and the desire to have a free, if irregular relationship had been wreaking havoc and even causing wars ever since Helen of Troy – and the history of the Western world is littered with tragic love stories such as Tristan and Isolde or Romeo and Juliet, not to mention the heart-breaking case of poor Millie McGilligan and her married solicitor lover Norman Gladwell in Ipswich. But of course these tragedies simply confirmed the rightness of the official family order and the naturalness of the unequal relationship between men and women which, being natural, had to be provided with an intellectual and moral justification. And by you-know-who.

By men?
Who else?! So if women were in a subordinate role, why was that? Because they were inferior to men, obviously, and were indeed puzzlingly inadequate. This oversized old guy Saint Thomas Aquinas – though admittedly he was nicknamed 'the dumb Sicilian ox' – decided after earnest theological thought that 'woman was defective and misbegotten'. In Islamic society women were kept in order rather like children and on occasion, as with children, beaten for their own good – there are examples like Afghanistan even today. So you prevented women from being educated or playing a part in public affairs and then – surprise surprise – marvelled at their inadequacy.

Sounds like a neat trick.
But there was an even neater trick. So you had the status quo

threatened by the disruptive force of sex, didn't you? And whose fault was that? Obviously, since women played such a secondary role and were relatively powerless, it could only be the fault of…?

Men?
Absolutely not! How could you think such a thing?! It was obviously the women who *caused* all the trouble, who *attracted* men's desires and were therefore the source of the evil – after all, it was Eve, wasn't it, who started it all off by feeding Adam that forbidden apple in the garden of Eden? So man was 'born in sin', born of sexual activity, born of woman. For the Christian church the torments of sex – which were real enough to leave poor Saint Augustine pleading with God to make him chaste, but please please please please God 'not just yet' – represented the ultimate sin, the temptation of the Devil, the way to damnation. Which is why women had to be controlled and protected not just from the ways of the world, but from themselves.

But it's not like that now, you said?
Well, the industrial revolution began to bring women into the work force and therefore into contact with the world beyond the home, while the increase in prosperity created a growing group of middle-class women who aspired to an education that would enable them to play a part in public affairs. So at the end of the 19th century, you began to see women trying to break into the university system with their own colleges, like Girton and Newnham in Cambridge or Somerville and Lady Margaret Hall in Oxford.

That was progress, wasn't it?
Progress that was fought by the male establishment every inch of the way. The Church of England was particularly inclined to see this development as heralding the end of civilization, with one reverend gentleman calling Girton College an 'infidel place' and an Oxford theologian describing Lady Margaret Hall as 'running counter to the wisdom and experience of all the centuries of Christendom'. So arguments put forward to resist this feminine onslaught were many and various, beginning with the moral scandal involved. For how could you bring young ladies away from home into such close contact with often boisterous young men and not foresee the dire consequences?

And were the consequences dire?
Of course not – Girton was deliberately situated four miles from Cambridge to keep the wolves away and anyway the young ladies were chaperoned. But then there were the worrying medical issues. For women just weren't up to the strain of such studies. Too much mental effort was said to be bad for their health, especially during their menstrual periods, and in any case their brains, since they were 8% smaller than men's brains, were just not up to studying hard 'masculine' subjects like mathematics or science or Ancient Greek. Mathematics in particular was the most prestigious degree for men at that time, so how do you think they reacted when a young lady called Philippa Fawcett of Newnham College trounced the men in the mathematics tripos, the final exam at Cambridge, in 1890?

3. THE YOU IN THE MIRROR — Male or female

They had to be impressed.
Impressed to the point of seeing no end to this feminist avalanche that was threatening the status quo, especially since women were beginning to demand not only to be educated like the men, but to have a say in how the laws governing their lives were established – to have the Vote, for heaven's sake! Poor creatures incapable of understanding the workings of politics and parliament seeking to turn society upside-down by having the Vote! But in the twenty years before the First World War broke out in 1914, these poor creatures fought their own war with the government and the police to obtain it.

And was it a rough war?
Not at first it wasn't. The behaviour of these Suffragettes as they were called was initially very ladylike and provoked little more than mild amusement. But the frustration grew, and the tone changed markedly after a couple of them were thrown out of a meeting in Manchester at which Winston Churchill was speaking. Arrested for obstruction, they raised the stakes by refusing to pay the fine and so forcing the authorities to send them to prison, which started the pattern whereby they heckled at meetings, were roughly expelled and went on hunger strike when they were thrown into prison. But when all this was regarded by the political establishment and the Church of England as little more than a public nuisance, these ladylike Suffragettes decided to be a little less ladylike.

So what did they do?
They did plenty. They firebombed politicians' houses,

burned down churches, smashed shop windows in Oxford Street, refused to pay their taxes, chained themselves to the railings of Buckingham Palace and a few other things. But it took more than that to win the gender war on voting. It took Emily Davidson to fling herself under the King's horse and be killed at the 1913 Derby, which gave a tragic dimension to the struggle, and it also took the First World War which broke out the following year.

Did they fight?
No, they weren't allowed to, but they declared patriotically that they would suspend their campaign while the war lasted. And since women came to play an important part in the war by taking over the jobs of men at the front, the climate of opinion changed to the extent that, though they did not have equal voting rights with men until 1928, the franchise was extended in 1918 to married women over thirty. Which chimed with what was happening in other countries, with Germany, for example, granting women the vote in 1918 and the US doing so in 1920. Others, like France and Italy, followed suit after World War II and many countries around the world have now granted women voting rights – even including Saudi Arabia in 2015. And with Oxford following the trend by awarding degrees to women by 1920 and Cambridge offering at least an equivalent diploma by 1921 – though not on equal terms with men until 1948 – you can see the direction of travel.

So the Suffragettes would be happy, would they?
Up to a point. You can't quite say that women have achieved

equality in politics – in parliaments across the world their representation is still less than 25% – or that in many areas they have achieved equal wages. And it is not simply that the power still largely lies with men, but that the gender confusion in this transitional period is such that women still often tend to grade themselves according to male values – with little girls pretty in pink, teenage girls thinking if might seem unfeminine to study mathematics and science, or finding themselves judged by comparison with half-starved professional models, and so on. But at least the situation is more open, and people are freer to try to define themselves in their own way.

Even so, I'd still find it easier to be a man.
Probably. Although either way, of course, there are the constraints that come from your inheritance.

4. YOUR PHYSICAL INHERITANCE
Luck of the draw

OK, so you will have inherited from your family certain features, apart from sex or gender, that mark you out from other people.

That makes me even more 'special'. Do I have to be this 'special'?
Well yes, because you may have red hair when those around you have black or blonde hair, or mysteriously deep green eyes when everybody else seems to have blue or brown eyes, or possibly strikingly prominent cheekbones, unusually small feet, long fingers and funny ears.

With red hair, unusually small feet and funny ears, would that perhaps make me a bit too special?
Ah, but that's just the point. Since you're special you aspire to be different, a real individual – to be yourself in fact. So we'd better see just how much room for manoeuvre you've got. Let's start with your vertical axis.

4. YOUR PHYSICAL INHERITANCE — Luck of the draw

My what?!
Your height. Of course, people have got taller over thousands of years because of selection and even over the past half century because of better nutrition. And it does vary from one society to another. For example, the average height of young women in the Netherlands is 5'7" (169.9cm) as opposed to 4'8" (142.2cm) in Bolivia, with comparable figures for men for the same countries being 6' (183cm) and 5'3" (160cm).

Quite a difference!
There are advantages to being tall, quite apart from not having to stand on a chair to reach the top shelf or replace a light bulb. You tend, at least if you are male, not to get bullied at school, you have an advantage in various sports, and you stand out in social and professional gatherings. You have better job opportunities – and not only in modelling. Tall people, partly because they tend to be more self-confident, have generally been seen as having a superior pedigree, as being more intelligent and more competent. And while you're being looked up to, you can have a better career, earn more money, and be convinced in all innocence that you deserve to.

Looks like a nice pitch.
If you're a man, other things being equal – not, between you and me, that things ever are equal – you tend to be more attractive to women since you look more able to protect and provide. And if you're a good actor who is dark and handsome but short, you can wear lifts in your shoes like

Tom Cruise or be filmed at an angle that will make you look tall, like Humphrey Bogart partnered with the taller Ingrid Bergman in *Casablanca,* so that the women in the audience can sigh and feel at one with the heartthrob you're pretending to be. And I say nothing about Alan Ladd.

Who on earth is Alan Ladd?
Before your time – and mine! But he was this short yellow-haired film star, who had false hair stuck on his chest to make him look tough, and who was made to tower over his taller female co-star by having him stand on a banana box or else, as they strolled along dreamily together into a golden sunset, by having her walk in a specially dug trench – and it doesn't get more romantic than that!

So it was all a lie?
Let's just say it was an expectation, even an aspiration. In short, a convention.

So for women it would be the same thing as for men, but the other way round?
Pretty much. There are certain advantages to being tall for women as well, of course. Not only can you look like a model, be commanding in group situations and have better career prospects, but your clothes hang better, you can have legs up to your eyebrows and you don't have to wreck your feet and ankles by wearing high heels. However…

There's a downside?
Indeed. Unlike boys, you're more at risk of being bullied

at school, you'd better not be taller than your boss and, above all, you may frighten away a lot of desirable partners or, even worse, attract weirdos and shortarses mainly interested in swanning around with conspicuous trophy girlfriends.

So what do you do?
You recognise that, while you may wish to see yourself as an individual rather than just being like everybody else, you are in practice operating within conventional constraints. It might be too uncomfortable being a 6' tall woman in Bolivia or a 4'3" woman in the Netherlands, and you wouldn't want to be taken either for your tall boyfriend's daughter or for your short boyfriend's big sister, would you?

I suppose not.
And if you're a guy 5' tall you can forget about being a star at basketball or the high jump or being a rugby forward. It may be that Danny Devito managed to make an acting career out of being 4'10" tall, but that's just the exception that proves the rule, isn't it? There are conventional limits and not only you, but other people will be aware of them.

So size matters.
And that's only the vertical dimension of yourself that will affect your social and personal situation, though since you can't do anything to make yourself shorter or taller, it's the easy one to deal with. But then there's the horizontal axis: your girth.

Whether you're too fat or too thin?
Yes, but mostly whether you're too fat. Of course, there have been societies where it was fashionable to be plump, where it showed that you had the wealth and the leisure to be plump, where – as with the voluptuous nudes in the paintings of Rubens, say – it was sexy to be plump. But now…

You're not supposed to be plump?
Now you've got to be slim. That has been the great obsession of our time, the one that gives rise to a slimming industry that spews out millions of slimming books, slimming articles, slimming ads and slimming apps, not to mention slimming support groups, slimming recipes and so-called slimming foods that will keep you eating, so that you will go on trying pathetically to eat yourself slim and worrying yourself to death about not being slim without realising that your chances, frankly, are…

Slim?
It's easy to see where all this comes from, of course. As society has developed, food has become more available, indeed in today's cities it has become available in supermarkets and coffee shops at every hour of the day and night. It costs money, of course, but then that's the point. The food industry with its constant publicity churns out a multitude of fatty and sugary processed foods, which pile on the pounds and keep you coming back for more. Even the so-called healthy items, like fruit juices, are loaded with sugar to leave you innocently piling on more weight. And that's not all.

4. YOUR PHYSICAL INHERITANCE — Luck of the draw

There's more?
Yes, because the constant availability of ready-to-eat and mostly junk food means that people are eating at all hours of the day in the street, in the office, in the bus, in the library or on the escalators in the Underground – and generally with a high street coffee shop coffee that's as much sugar as coffee. And since work itself has become less physical in character, since we spend half of our time sitting in front of a computer or TV screen – where the programmes are regularly interrupted with ads inviting us to eat – and since we also have microwaves that can immediately whip up something to eat, we don't get around on foot as much as people used to.

So nobody gets slim?
The only people who seem to keep slim are the waiters in coffee shops and the delivery men who rush around serving up all that fattening stuff to make us fat. Which feeds into the issues that arise from being overweight, the first being obviously your health. If you're so fat – to stick to the technical term – that you've lost touch with your southern hemisphere and can't lean forward to see your feet without falling flat on your face, you've got a problem.

An oversize problem, by the sound of it!
It's not just that being fat will leave you tired, breathless and unable to run for the bus. It can involve a list of medical conditions as long as your plump arm, including back problems, high blood pressure, coronary heart disease, diabetes, kidney disease, fertility problems and – if you're

still up for it – erectile dysfunction. I could go on till dinner time…

And you sound as though you intend to!
But that should be enough to make the point. In some cases there may be a genetic factor, in others it may result from having obese parents – if they were poor and ate junk food – but in most cases it is due to the current lifestyle and to the constant pressures of the publicity machine. The fatness food industry has got you in its grip. And that's not counting the other aspect of being overweight…

Your appearance?
Exactly. When you look at photographs of blank-faced anorexic models like stick insects advancing rhythmically along the catwalk with one high-heeled foot carefully placed in front of the other – who ever walked like that, apart from trapeze artists?! – you may feel unattractive. You may have difficulty finding clothes to fit you, you may feel envious of your friends, you may lose self-esteem, you may feel that love and life have passed you by…

Sad…!
And just as the fatness food industry had you in its grip, so the vast slimming industry – for of course they get you from both ends, like the fatness-fitness industry – threatens to get its claws into you. And this despite the great open secret that slimming books don't prevent you from getting fat, that buying the book tends to be a way of evading rather than confronting the problem and that, when eventually you

waddle over to survey your long row of slimming books, you will reflect despairingly, God help you, that you have lost more money than fat.

You've mentioned God again. Is he fat?
What?! No no, that's something different, we'll get on to that later. Where was I…?

People in despair about being fat. Not knowing what you should do.
I can tell you what you should do. Take the possible health consequences seriously, go to see the doctor for a check-up and, beyond that, do the obvious things: avoid fatty and sugary foods, eat more fruit and fibre, cut out snacks, concentrate on what you are eating and chew more slowly. As for exercise, try to fit walking into the normal day's pattern rather than self-consciously and reluctantly 'going for a walk' and, if none of that works, get yourself a dog – the younger and bigger the better. And, needless to say…

Don't overfeed the dog?
Quite. But, above all, don't make a fetish out of slimming. Don't keep weighing yourself and inspecting yourself in the mirror, don't mark your progress every day on the bathroom wall, don't join slimming support groups, don't bore your friends or your neighbours or the old lady in the bus queue to death by talking about it. All you are doing is returning to a balance between food intake and exercise that was normal for thousands of years, so don't make a religion out of it.

'Religion'? But doesn't religion mean...?
Stop trying to get me into religion, I said we'd get into all that later! I'm talking about how you'd deal with a weight problem.

But if none of all that worked?
Then you might have to ask yourself whether you're not seeing the real problem, whether your concern about being overweight isn't masking depression, dissatisfaction with your studies or your job, or with a failure to connect with people – for which the answer might be to get out there, join groups and be actively involved in things beyond your own little concerns.

Which mightn't be as easy as you make it sound?
No, but it's better than trying to short-circuit the problem through cosmetic surgery, which is so often only a form of self-harm. Of course it might well be suitable in instances of disfigurement or other medically approved cases. It might also be understandable if you were trying desperately to get back into employment in hard economic times and you were looking for a job where appearance was an issue – like those fortyish tough guys who had H-A-T-E or B-O-L-L-O-C-K-S tattooed on their foreheads when they were twenty and haven't found it easy to get smiley customer-friendly jobs as hotel porters or assistants in clothes shops.

I can see that might be difficult.
If you're a man worried about hair loss, you might do better to shave off what's left and look macho-executive rather than

get the kind of transplant – so obvious in well-known actors, footballers or television commentators – that would just make people slightly sorry for you. And if you are a woman, you don't want to end up like those middle-aged Barbie Doll women in California with identical faces and identical fixed smiles like alien creatures in one of those ghastly sci-fi films featuring ghosts, avatars or vampires.

Sounds frightening.
Anyway, it may be quite naïve to believe that smaller breasts and a smaller bum – not to mention a restyled vagina – can transform your career and relationships. Many men, who of course have their own insecurities, not only respond well to plump women, but see beyond these attributes to the person involved. And just as short men often compensate by being funnier or more ambitious – sometimes to the point of becoming successful comics or emperors – so plump women tend to compensate by having a livelier, more jolly personality.

That's reassuring.
And rightly so. For we may have these stereotypes of the tall dark handsome man and the slim and statuesque woman, but these remain ideal images for those glossy magazines in the hairdresser's which depend commercially on giving you enough anxieties and insecurities to make you want to go out and buy some more glossy magazines. But they play little part in the complexity of real relationships, which involve other values such as sympathy, intelligence and reliability. Beauty, between you and me, and don't quote me…

Don't worry, I won't.
Beauty, as some beautiful women will tell you, can be a bit isolating in that it can frighten some desirable men away. In the end, it's not so much about looks as about personality. You can't live in an online or glossy magazine fantasyland. You may want to be 'different' and not just 'the same as everybody else', but in practice life goes on between these two extremes. 'Special' or not, you've got to live in the real world.

Yes, well, if it's the only world I've got.
Meanwhile, there's one inherited trait in addition to height and girth that I haven't mentioned.

And what's that?
Colour. Since we're a pretty colourful species, you may be born white or black or brown or yellow or duck egg green. And it makes life simpler if you are born in the right place.

But you can't, can you?
No, and that's the problem. If you're born black in Nigeria or yellow in China, nobody notices, but if you born black or yellow in Europe or Russia, say, you have to live with the sense of being different. And though with the globalization of trade and information through television and the Web, nobody is astonished these days to see somebody who looks different…

It can make life complicated?
Exactly. Of course people, especially where they feel vulnerable and threatened by change, have always tended

4. YOUR PHYSICAL INHERITANCE — Luck of the draw

to define themselves in contradistinction to other people, so you get him-and-her, us-and-them, Left-versus-Right, locals-versus-foreigners, Protestants-versus-Catholics, Sunni-versus-Shia, East-versus-West and, in our fevered imagination, humans versus aliens, ghosts, vampires, robots, giant squids, or whatever. It's as though you only really know who you are when you know who you're not – who you're different from. And since you can be different from others in a whole variety of ways...

You can be prejudiced in a whole variety of ways?
Yes, you can be prejudiced against gays, immigrants, Jews, Muslims, Catholics, benefit seekers, the rich, the old, the young, the disabled or that red-haired git of a dog-owner at the end of the street – you name it! Of course, there are laws against discriminating on grounds of age, gender, disability, religion or race in regard to jobs, education or public services, but even in what aspires to be post-racial Britain – with its capital London perhaps the most multicultural city in the world – there is still a degree of discrimination, however subtle or indirect. And of course, at any interview your colour, as opposed to your religion, sexual inclination or political views...

Is immediately obvious?
We're a long way from the old days in Britain, when you had boarding houses with signs saying: 'No Dogs, no Blacks, no Irish'. And we're a long way from the Ku Klux Klan and the hangings of blacks in the United States, even if we still see almost routine police violence like the killing of George

Floyd in Minneapolis in 2020, or the unacknowledged or even unconscious racism underlying nationalist movements like Brexit. However, black and other ethnic minorities are still at a disadvantage in regard to employment, housing and consequently health – as was seen clearly during the Covid-19 pandemic – as well as in their treatment by the justice system. Now you might think it's just a matter of social class, that racial discrimination is experienced only by the poor, who live in deprived areas...

I don't think I would think that.
No, because even those middle-class ethnic minority students who graduate from the best universities tend not to have equal outcomes as regards employment. And when it comes to public housing in Britain, which is in dramatically short supply in any case, minority applicants can find themselves excluded on indirect grounds such as length of residence. I'm afraid discrimination on grounds of colour won't end this year or next.

So when will it end?
When we intermingle and all end up the same colour as one big family, I suppose.

And what colour would that be?
Cappuccino, I imagine – without the bubbles. But meanwhile you'll have to contend with your own family.

Which would be white and middle-class, would it?
I didn't say that, did I?

No you didn't. You didn't have to somehow.
Not being cheeky again, are you?

No no. I wouldn't dream of it!

---

5. FAMILIES

And everybody has one

You're happy to continue then, are you?

Of course.
OK, so you take a long time to grow up and therefore you have a family. Even if you're adopted and have alternative parental figures, you have a family. And even if you're an orphan entirely on your own, you have at least the memory of a family or some sort of shadow awareness of family. The family is the micro unit of society, so whether you like it or not you have a family.

You're hinting that it's not all happy families?
Most are happy, I suppose, even if some are not, but happy or not happy, the family tie tends to be inescapable. It may even, ironically, be stronger and more demanding if you are stuck with an unhappy family. Although, as the playwright Oscar Wilde put it, 'after a good dinner you can forgive anybody, even your own relations'. Not that his family every quite forgave him!

5. FAMILIES — And everybody has one

Why not?
Well he was gay, which didn't entirely help the marriage, especially since it was also illegal at that time, so he had a spell in Reading gaol and ended up dying in a dingy hotel in Paris complaining about the wallpaper.

So what was wrong with the wallpaper?
I don't know, he probably thought it was vulgar or petit-bourgeois or something. The French are funny about wallpaper – either it's supremely elegant or disastrously ugly. But why go on about the wallpaper? He didn't die because of the wallpaper!

Sorry, but it was you who mentioned it.
All right, but we're straying off the point. Where were we?

Happy families and unhappy families.
Yes, well the great Russian writer Leo Tolstoy had views about all that – from his own experience I may say.

So was his own family life happy or unhappy?
It was a bloody nightmare, as it happens – a lot more War than Peace. Anyway, he said famously that 'happy families are all alike; every unhappy family is unhappy in its own way'.

What does that mean exactly?
I'm not sure it means all that much, now that you ask – beyond saying that there are a lot of reasons why families can be unhappy. Like illness, sexual incompatibility, lack of money or status, differences of religious or social views – as

in Tolstoy's case – or whatever. Which is only to bring out the obvious.

Which is?
That the family is just a cell in the social body, that it is in constant interaction with that body and that it changes as society changes. We live in history, don't we?

If you say so.
So the family structure in the pre-industrial era reflected its ability to make a living for its members, which in turn was affected by such factors as geography, climate, the fertility of the soil and whether there was peace or war. And up to the end of the nineteenth century the essential source of wealth was land.

So you had to own land?
Either that or you had to work somebody else's land for a living, as most had to do. And the household structure depended largely on how well off the family was. In poorer families, you tended to have marriages taking place later, limiting the number of children though even then some had to be farmed out to earn their keep as servants to richer families. If you were the eldest son, and therefore due to take over on your father's death, you could afford to marry, but other sons might simply be too poor to marry, and the daughters were dependent on whoever might or might not come along to pick them from the shelf. Up to fifteen percent of the population were never able to afford to get married and set up a household.

5. FAMILIES — And everybody has one

Not a great scene then?
Especially when you think that life was hard, that children often died in infancy and that people didn't live as long as we do. And on top of that, with little or nothing in the way of medical care or education, the family had to act as a kind of insurance society, coping not only with feeding and clothing its members but with looking after the sick and the elderly. But the situation changed with the shift towards working in factories in larger industrial towns...

So things got better?
Initially they got worse in some ways since the working conditions in industries such as steel or mining or cotton were very harsh. But, as prosperity increased, the burden of schooling and the care of the sick passed gradually to public institutions, while food production was also becoming industrialized. And in this situation the family became a tighter, more nuclear unit consisting essentially of the couple and their children, enjoying more privacy yet also a greater opening to this new urban society in which they found themselves. Of course, there were other, negative factors holding this nuclear family together...

I'm getting used to 'negative factors'! So what were they?
Relative poverty, the dependent situation of women and the consequent near-impossibility of divorce. Even so, with children beginning to get some schooling rather than being little wage earners, and with women working in factories, getting more access to life outside the home and getting sufficient recognition by the end of World War One, as we saw...

To get the Vote?
As well as some movement towards equal opportunity in education, the situation gradually improved even through two World Wars until the family pattern began to change yet again…

I knew it!
Well then you know that it changed with the eruption on to the scene – in the 1950s in the US and a decade later in the UK – of you-know-who.

I don't know that I do know this you-know-who.
It was the terrible teenager, an American invention initially. Until then children were supposed to be obedient to the point of 'being seen and not heard', but with increasing prosperity after World War II they began to be seen and heard with a vengeance. For they had cars and girlfriends or boyfriends and lots of time on their hands – enough to feel that the oldies didn't understand them, that they were 'different', that the world was all wrong, and all that. They were rebels without a cause, as you might say.

So what happened to them?
They grew up, went into jobs, had kids who felt that they were 'different', that their parents didn't understand them, that the world was all wrong and all that carry-on. It's a standard developmental phase in a rapidly changing world.

So what was changing?
Damned nearly everything, really. After a giant World War

II and the shift towards globalization of the economy and of information – with every part of the planet coming alive on TV – people were beginning to have to live with an awareness of the whole wide world rather than of their own cosy little bit of it. And a lot of unquestioned assumptions began gradually to fall away.

Like what?
Like the automatic assumption that the man went out to work and the woman stayed at home to look after the kids, do the shopping, bake cakes, and look pretty and welcoming for his return. For women were now more educated and eager to get out of the kitchen to exploit their talents. And indeed there were opportunities available, especially since the shift away from heavy industry and the growth of the tertiary sector of the economy meant jobs to which women's greater dexterity and social skills were particularly suited. And this began to change the power relationship between the sexes.

Power?
Yes, it led to a better *balance* of power. So long as women were financially dependent on men, they were also legally and emotionally dependent. This meant in practice that they depended on getting married and that, if they were unhappy, divorce was normally unaffordable and considered scandalous – and even if you could afford it, it was not only stressful, expensive and long drawn out, but you ran the risk of losing your children. However, changes in the law have made it easier for women to get a divorce on reasonable

terms, so that the UK has now one of the highest divorce rates in Europe. But then many people get divorced in order to remarry, in defiance of the view of the good Dr Johnson, who said famously that second marriages represented 'the triumph of hope over experience'.

So did he have a bad second marriage?
He was only married once, to a widow twice his age who thought her second marriage to this toyboy, though he fidgeted and grunted a lot with Tourette's syndrome, was wonderful. But you mustn't drag me off the point. Which is that the traditional foundations of marriage were crumbling. The proportion of the population with strong religious beliefs had fallen and the general attitude to sex – especially since it was no longer a high-risk activity after the advent of the Pill – was relaxed to the point that the poet Philip Larkin could write that 'sexual intercourse began in nineteen sixty-three, along with the Beatles and the first LP.' And since it has become pretty routine for couples to live together without feeling that they have to get married, you can imagine what sort of a situation we have today.

I'm not sure I can!
I don't blame you, for the situation of the family today is more than a little complicated. In addition to the traditional married couple with children you have stepfamilies, where one or both parents have previously been married – and there are more and more of these, since almost half of all marriages in the UK today are in fact re-marriages. You have single parent families, whether by

design or because the parents' marriage has broken down. You have civil partnership between same sex couples, with or without children. Then you have millions of couples living apart, either because they don't want to commit to living together, because they tried that and it failed, because they have family obligations elsewhere, because they have jobs in different areas of the country, or whatever. And that's not counting children living with aunts and uncles or grandparents.

So what does all that add up to?
It adds up to the fact that there are now more unmarried than married adults in the UK, that over half of children are now being born to unmarried parents, that we have one of the higher rates of pregnancy in Western Europe – and that the traditional sequence of engagement, marriage and baby is now being turned by some on its head, with the engagement coming last. And you're about to ask me if all this is good or bad.

Well, I wasn't, actually.
Well you should be! The answer, I suppose, is that it's generally good, but that it brings problems. It's good for women in that they gain greater independence – that they are no longer in effect having to trade sex for marriage and financial support – but then freedom can be demanding. It's not easy for the single parent who has to combine job and motherhood, especially given the high cost of housing and childcare. And for women generally there is now the problem of when to have children, with the need to establish

themselves in a career leading many to put off motherhood later and later. This at a time when families are more dispersed geographically than ever before and when people are also living longer, so that a woman – and it is mostly the woman – may now find herself having to care for ageing parents as well as young children, coping with two generations at once. All this means a profound change for society.

So where do men fit into all this?
Good question. They are obviously having to adjust, but the traditional sexist attitudes linger on. Women are now present in management positions, even if they remain in a minority. So it can be difficult for some men – especially since manliness was traditionally associated with manual work in the now disappearing heavy industrial sector – to feel comfortable with a female boss or to find themselves less educated and earning less than their female partner. It is an unhappy fact that crude sexist attitudes, now made more serious by the vicious practice of trolling, are still present in our schools, where girls afraid of seeming too clever often just 'let the boys do the talking'.

So how do the children make out with all these changes to the family structure?
It's mixed, I suppose. For some it might be a relief to escape the closeness of the traditional nuclear family, but a young child may feel confused or betrayed and may not get on at all with a new stepfather. In any event, however the family is structured, it still acts as a microcosm of society at large. Children have to define themselves in relation to

the adults around them and, given the complexity of family dynamics…

That's not always easy…?
As we are about to see.

6. FAMILY DYNAMICS
Don't get mangled in the machine

I suppose I have to start by quoting Philip Larkin again.

Who is this Larkin guy who thought sex didn't exist until 1963? Well, it didn't exist too much for him! He was a grumpy and gloomy hermit of a librarian in Hull who hid a failure to connect with people and enjoy life behind a stylized cynicism. Anyway, he wrote this famous poem about parents and children, which begins elegantly as follows:

> They fuck you up, your mum and dad,
> They may not mean to, but they do.
> They fill you with the faults they had,
> And add some extra, just for you.

But then he goes on to say that 'they were fucked up in their turn' and concludes that, through the family, 'man hands on misery to man'. Of course, there are parodies of this by more optimistic poets: one by Richard Kell beginning 'They *buck*

6. FAMILY DYNAMICS   Don't get mangled in the machine

you up, your mum and dad' and another by Adrian Mitchell beginning sweetly 'They *tuck* you up, your mum and dad'. But the poem would hardly be so famous if it did not touch on a sensitive area.

So what were his own mum and dad like?
Well, for a start it was apparently a dark gloomy household with few visitors. His mother was nervous, depressed and self-pitying, which was perhaps understandable since his father was a self-made man with Fascist sympathies who attended Nazi rallies in Nuremberg and had a swastika on the wall in his office. It's almost painfully obvious to see why Philip adopted the racist views of the admired strong partner, his father, and did not have a high view of women. That he was educated at home until the age of eight may not have helped, but his family seems to have done him few favours.

Except that it helped him to become a famous poet?
Yes, if you think that was adequate compensation! But it illustrates how many see the family, with its classic mother, father, sons, daughters structure as a kind of four-cornered boxing match. Of course, the nature of the relationship between the parents may well complicate the picture, as will their level of education and cultural beliefs, the number of children, or special factors such as illness or the early death of a parent. Also, in the new unconventional family structures there may be a surrogate father or mother, which can create special problems. Nevertheless, speculation has centred upon the basic relationships of father-son, father-

daughter, mother-son and mother-daughter. And inevitably so, because all of them can be problematic. So where do we begin?

With the father-son relationship, I suppose.
Patriarchal already, are you?! Still, it's logical given the patriarchal history of the family, although the father's dominance has been eroded by a whole sequence of changes. When industrial society took him to work outside the home, he became the largely absent figure whose status was determined by the external standard of how he rated as money-earner. His authority has also tended to be diminished where rapid technological progress leaves him with a son more sophisticated and attuned to a changing world than himself.

I'm beginning to feel sorry for this fellow!
You're right, but you should also feel sorry for the son, for sons do need fathers, which is why there is such an attempt today to get fathers – whose long working days often only let them see their kids at the weekend – to push the pram around and do more in the home. For, whatever the generation gap, there is a basic power conflict that has to be resolved.

Another power conflict?
Yes, because the son has to grow up – and in practice has to grow up by asserting himself against this figure who has always represented the manhood the son must try to achieve. So while as a small child he may have played happily with

the father, he tends as a teenager to become rebellious in the attempt to get treated on equal terms. This is a fight which he has to win if he is to grow up and it has to seem to be a real fight. So it is up to the father to understand and to put up a real fight – but just enough to let the son win on points and be granted equal status as an independent adult. It is a tricky game, without explicit rules, but if it is played properly father and son can really begin to get to know each other as people with ordinary strengths and weaknesses. Now, as for the mother-son relationship…

Which I expect you'll tell me is equally tricky?
Yes, but in a different way. Mothers tend generally to have a greater emotional investment in children than fathers, although that old Greek philosopher Aristotle suggested mischievously that it might be because they were more certain that they were their own children. However, the love of a mother for her son is generally believed to be the deepest love of all and, rather mysteriously, more than her love for a daughter, even though she has borne them in the same way. This may be because by having a son rather than a daughter she is achieving a full male-female fusion, or because sons have been seen as more important within the patriarchal system, or because, as Richard Dawkins suggests, there is an unconscious evolutionary drive to ensure that through the son her genes will live on after her. One way or the other, it is so profound that, if the mother fails to detach herself in good time, this may lead to a weak 'mummy's boy' unable to achieve full independence – or even to an unhealthily close relationship of the oedipal variety…

The what?
After this oddball Oedipus, a mythical Greek character who killed his father and married his mother. But of course he didn't mean to…

I'm glad to hear it!
Then you'll be glad to hear that it doesn't happen all that often.

So there's actually some good news!
Absolutely. For to the growing boy the mother represents womanhood as the father represents manhood and a close bond of love and respect between them produces enormous benefits. It is she who can instil emotional intelligence, teach him to recognise his own feelings and those of others, steer him away from the aggressive tough-guy male stereotypes that unhappy teenagers tend self-protectively to adopt and, indeed, provide him with the communication and social skills he will need in the modern working world. And, needless to say, she can provide him with an example of femininity which will lead him to respect and sympathize with the girls he will meet.

But what about these girls? It sounds as though they don't do so well.
Well, it's true that historically, because of their secondary status, they tended to be treated as charming little things but not taken too seriously, and it's a fact that even up to today the father tends to be absent from their lives more than the mother from the sons'. But the father too has a

fundamental role in that he still represents the big wide world and provides an example of masculinity, especially in his attitude to her mother, that will certainly influence her. She needs to feel that she can trust him, that he will protect and provide and that, as she goes through the often delicate teenage years and finds herself viewed as a sexual object, he loves and respects her as a person. Fathers who are emotionally less articulate may be embarrassed by the conflicts that arise in these years and withdraw to the extent of seeming indifferent, failing to understand the importance of their role. But where they demonstrate their love and concern, they provide the girl with the self-belief she needs to advance successfully into adulthood. And it may even be, as we move towards greater gender equality, that rather than diminishing, their importance is greater than ever.

Is that not a bit paradoxical?
It is, but if you want to see something paradoxical look at the relationship between mother and daughter. The reasons for this are of course perfectly obvious…

Not to me they aren't.
Well in the first place they're both female, with each seeing a reflection of herself in the other, the mother wishing to realise herself in the daughter, the daughter seeing the mother initially as the role model. And the relationship tends to be more intense than that of father and son for several reasons. One is simply that, as the primary caregiver, the mother tends to be more present in the home than the father. Another is that, while fathers and sons tend to

communicate by doing manly things together and either exchanging grunts or talking about anything but themselves, women and daughters tend to negotiate by expressing their feelings and opening up to each other, in short by talking. And though male members of the family often wonder how they can have so much to talk about, the social pressures on girls mean that they really do have more to talk about than boys.

Like what?
Like all those things that are subject to fashion and change, such as their hairstyle, their clothes, their makeup, their nails or their tattoos. And of course the risks that don't apply to boys in the same way, of unwanted attention on public transport, of coming home alone late at night, or of getting pregnant. There are plenty of things for mothers and daughters to talk about – and therefore to disagree over, even to compete over and, since by talking they expose their vulnerability, to lay themselves open to hurt. So you get the standard complaints from the unhappy daughter that the mother never really listened to her properly, that she always criticized her choice of clothes or boyfriends, that she wanted her to be someone that she didn't want to be, and so on – mirrored of course by the complaints of the mother, who may have had much less freedom when going through the same stage herself, that the daughter wouldn't listen to advice, didn't understand the risks, was giving the family a bad name, or whatever. And since the novel itself is largely becoming a feminine form, there is an avalanche of stories about the fraught relationship of mothers and daughters.

6. FAMILY DYNAMICS — Don't get mangled in the machine

So what's the paradox?
It's the paradox of the separation involved in growing up, I suppose. The daughter has to maintain the emotional bond with this mother who represented femininity while yet distancing herself from it in order to be independent, and to do so while minimizing the hurt that this may involve. The mother, similarly, has to try to maintain the bond while letting the daughter go. It's asking quite a lot at a time when social norms and moral assumptions have been changing markedly, but most mothers and daughters appear to manage it.

And if they don't?
Then they should try to understand the pressures of each other's situation, recognise like Philip Larkin that the parents didn't mean to do harm, recognise that life is short and – guess what – forgive each other.

And perhaps in the process forgive themselves?
A most interesting thought! Especially since there's a bit more to be forgiving and understanding about with families.

7. BIRTH ORDER

Do you fit the stereotype?

OK, so we've talked about different sorts of families and how to survive in the one you happen to land in, whether it's conventional, unconventional, nuclear, extended, single parent, stepfamily, lesbian, gay – or whatever.

Yeah, whatever!
And if that's not complicated enough for you, let's go on to the issue of the number of children in the family and the question of birth order. For of course there could be only one child or a dozen children involved, which means that you could be an only child, the oldest child, the youngest child, a middle child – either the second, third, fourth, ninth child or whatever...

Or whatever!
And to complicate things a little further let's not forget that you could also be a twin or a triplet or an adopted child, or the only boy among girls, or vice versa. Not to mention that the children might all be girls, or vice versa.

7. BIRTH ORDER — Do you fit the stereotype?

There seem to be a lot of vice versas! And you don't get a choice as to what kind of family you land in, do you?

No you don't. And, to add a few more variables, it could be a wealthy family or a poor family, an agnostic or a Christian or a Muslim family, or the children could be spaced out in different ways so that having a brother or sister ten years older, say, wouldn't be the same as having one only two years older. So when a big Viennese psychologist like Alfred Adler – who more or less invented the inferiority complex, by the way – says that there are standard personality characteristics deriving from your pecking order in the family, you might think that with so many family combinations possible he's…

Talking nonsense?

Not quite. But you might think, as other psychologists have argued, that he can at best be talking about stereotypes. On the other hand, stereotypes don't come from nowhere, they have developed over centuries out of people's perceptions of the power dynamics within families. And it's obvious that, whatever the composition of the family may be, you are bound to situate yourself in relation to the other members of it. And the important thing to recognise is that it's how you *feel* about your status, in the light of the particular family circumstances.

So how did this Adler fellow feel about his status?

Well, his own circumstances were that he had rickets as a small child and couldn't walk until he was four, when he caught pneumonia and overheard the doctor telling his father that he was going to die and, since he had already seen his younger brother die a year earlier, this was very bad news. However, he survived and, like many others who have seen early illness or death in the family, decided at once that he would go into medicine. This in itself suggests determination and he certainly became very competitive towards his older brother, who was some eighteen months his senior. Had this brother Sigmund been ten years older, there might have been no grounds for comparison, but the closeness in age was doubtless a factor.

So it's all in the detail?
Yes, but the need to establish your position in the family is real. Of course, if you're an only child or a single adopted child, there is no problem – you really are the one. Since your parents have no previous experience, they think you're wonderful, Lord help them…

'Lord help them'? Who's this Lord then?
Sorry, I was just using a standard expression…

It's God again, is it?
Oh, for heaven's sake, didn't I say we'd talk about that later?! Where was I?

I was an only child, and the parents think I'm wonderful.
So they may be over-protective to the point of spoiling you. You may behave and speak in a more adult way, adopt more readily your parents' values and be more conventionally ambitious. Since you have not had the corners knocked off you by having to deal with siblings, you may have difficulty

sharing and making friends. And if you're a boy with no sister, or a girl with no brother, you're at some disadvantage.

I don't think I'd fancy being an only child.
Then you mightn't fancy being the oldest child either, since it is a bit like being an only child lumbered with underlings. Not only are you treated more like an adult, but you're expected to share responsibility and set a good example. You may tend to model yourself on the father if you're a boy, or the mother if you are a girl, and develop a conservative and authoritarian outlook.

I don't think I'd fancy that either.
Maybe not. Even so, while we may be far beyond the old days of the landed family when the eldest son inherited the estate, the second son went into the army and the youngest son went into the church, poor devil, nevertheless the only child or the oldest child – the son in particular – still tends to be in a privileged position and to be the most ambitious and conventionally successful. So if you want to get yourself a big name like Richard Branson or Boris Johnson or JK Rowling, that might be the way to go. Unless you think you'd be more of a middle child, like Bill Gates, Madonna or Nelson Mandela – not that you can conclude much from a list of names, since you need to get into the fine detail.

So what's good, bad or middling about the middle child then?
Well let's suppose you were the middle child of a family of five. You have the oldest, aspirational sibling above you. Then you have above you the second sibling, who like Adler

might be close enough to the oldest to compete with him, and then we have the youngest: you. But that's only until two further siblings come along and you are stuck with being Piggy in the middle. You are freer insofar as you don't have the same pressures upon you as your two seniors, but you may feel you don't have a significant role. This may make you more adaptable, since you are likely to have to try to mediate between the older and younger ones, but it may well lead you to feel squeezed out and be more rebellious. At the very least, it may lead you to differentiate yourself from your more conventional seniors and be more adventurous in your interests and choice of career – if your seniors are stockbrokers or criminal lawyers, you may prefer to be an artist or guitarist.

That sounds more interesting.
Yes, though the money's not so good. But you're beginning to sound as though you'd like to be the youngest child. In fact, this might make you feel a bit inferior and you might dream – often unrealistically – of proving you're better than all of them put together, though your position as the youngest child is unlikely to help. You would have a special place as the 'baby' of the family, having not only a mummy and a daddy but all the older siblings playing at being little mummies and daddies and looking after you. This is of course a recipe for being spoilt and you may not only have a low sense of responsibility and expect to have everything done for you but be demanding and impatient if it is not. But then with all these people around you, you are likely to be outgoing and to use charm as a tactic in getting your own

way – in school you might be the class clown. You might lack the persistence to succeed in a conventional occupation, but you might well make it as an actor or performer or celebrity of some kind. So how does that grab you?

I'm not sure. It sounds fun but a bit risky. What else could I be?
You could be a twin.

And then there would be two of me?
It might look like that to other people, who might be unable to tell you apart, but it wouldn't feel like that to you. Of course, you could be a non-identical twin, who just happened to be born at the same time and who is easily distinguishable, while even with identical twins one is likely to be stronger or more active or in some other way slightly different from the other. In any event, there is a positive side in that you are never lonely for want of a companion, you complement each other in many ways, you attract a lot of warmth and attention, and you tend to be loyal to each other throughout life.

Sounds good.
Yes, but there are problems. For a start, small twins tend to invent their own way of communicating and can take longer than usual to speak correctly. But there are also identity problems. Whereas small children begin to achieve their own individuality around the age of three, twins achieve this collectively and then experience a certain tension as they try to establish themselves as separate individuals. The very closeness of the relationship can make this a painful

process, especially as they move into the teenage years. However, this can usually be managed with some delicate handling by the parents and the lifelong closeness of some identical twins, even when living far apart, is little short of miraculous.

I think I'd quite like to be a twin.
But you can't be one on your own, I'm afraid. Still, you could always be a boy in a family consisting only of boys – though you'd have no experience of girls, and it could be hard on the mother, who might have wanted a girl and be tempted to dress you up in frilly dresses to compensate. Or you could be a girl in a family of girls, where you would be left wondering about boys and the mother, who might have dreamt of having a boy, might be innocently tempted to dress you up in some correspondingly manly outfit.

So it might be easier to be a girl in a household of boys – or of course vice versa?
Yes, there's a lot of vice versa involved in all this. It might indeed be easier, with your brothers to protect you, but then you mightn't know whether to become a tomboy to fit in with the atmosphere or to differentiate yourself by becoming extravagantly feminine. And of course, if you were a boy in your vice versa situation, you might be led either to become effeminate or to pitch yourself as the alpha male of the family. Depending.

Depending on what?
Depending on the general character of the family and the

approach of the parents. For of course the family is a two-way relationship between parents and children and, as you may have noticed, we haven't yet said enough about the parental side of the equation. There are obviously particular circumstances that can colour the whole experience of the child.

Like what?
Like the parents separating or getting a divorce. This may be more and more common these days, but it can be extremely painful for children, who may not understand what is happening, may even feel it's partly their fault and may worry about their own future – and who may then have to adjust to a new family situation if one or other parent finds a new partner. This situation calls for delicate handling by the adults involved if the children are not to become withdrawn or depressed. And then you have other damaging situations.

You mean there's worse?!
I'm afraid so. You may have parents who are alcoholics or drug users, leading to a chaotic family situation which can leave the children insecure, frustrated and either angry or believing once again that it may somehow be their fault. They may find it difficult to make friends outside, if only out of embarrassment at feeling obliged to keep their family circumstances secret. And this overlaps with the family where a parent, more usually the father – so often because he is inarticulate and is relieving his own feelings – engages in physical or even sexual abuse.

So have you any more bad news?
Not really. It's true that families can also be affected by money worries or illnesses and that you can have tensions where the children may be shedding their parents' cultural beliefs, as regards religion, sex or politics. And it is fair to say that some parents are just not quite up to the job, whether because they are depressed or ill or left behind educationally by their children. In a rapidly changing world that is only to be expected and needs to be treated understandingly by the younger members. But in the end most families rub along pretty well.

I'm relieved to hear it!
That's not to say that there is no bickering or angry exchanges or hurt feelings or misunderstandings, but this can be the healthy rough-and-tumble of negotiation whereby each member finds his own place within the family and learns to respect that of others. In the end, the family is the privileged and protected place within which you learn how to live in society.

So your birth order is not that important after all?
It's important, but it can't just be viewed mechanically and seen as your destiny. It has to be seen in the context of a person's own particular situation and to understand that is to limit any damaging effects. And in any case the situation seems to be changing…

For the better?
Yes, old Adler himself thought that birth order differences

7. BIRTH ORDER — Do you fit the stereotype?

would tend to lessen as the old patriarchal family became more open and democratic. And there are various factors favouring such a change. With more equality between the sexes, the son is no longer automatically privileged as regards inheritance or access to education and employment. With the acceleration of technological change, the parents' knowledge and skills are rapidly superseded and it is often now the young who explain things to their parents. And with the whole wide world now available on a tablet or an iPhone, young people are more aware of what it is like in other families and, indeed, are often much more influenced in their views by their peers than by the parents.

So just how important is *birth order then?*
It's important, but not necessarily a destiny – and you can free yourself from any damaging effects so long as you understand it.

Good. I think I'd like to be the middle child in a family of three. Which is exactly what I am. How odd!

Isn't it though?!

8. WEALTH AND CLASS
Where are you on the ladder?

Well, some families are richer than others, a fact that will affect your life in all sorts of ways. So we'd better do what nice people are not supposed to do and talk about money.

Why should nice people not want to talk about money?
Depends on which nice people you're talking about. If you've got it, you don't want to reveal how much more you have than other people – so you consider it vulgar and low-class to talk about money. If you haven't got it, you don't want to reveal how much less you've got, so there's a polite conspiracy to avoid talking about money. Except that the conspiracy is beginning to break down.

Why is that?
Because people are beginning to notice the inequality in incomes in many countries, but particularly in Britain and the United States. While the average salary in the UK is around £35,000 for men and £30,000 for women, the

contrast in income between those at the top and those at the bottom of the income range is startling. Quite apart from the figures for earnings of stars or celebrities, who might of course have a short career span – in a recent year the footballer Harry Kane earned £10 million and the singer Adele pocketed £27 million – it's notable that the average earnings of the chief executives of the 100 largest companies on the London Stock Exchange, the so-called Footsie 100, is around £3.9 million.

Which means that one of those big salary earners on this Footsie thing is – let's see – worth about 110 male workers or 130 female workers?

Or worth about 100 architects, 120 primary teachers, 170 bus drivers or 200 waiters – though it depends what you mean by 'worth'. But I suppose it does indicate the values of a society where you see such a great discrepancy, especially since salary income is only half of the story. There is also wealth in the form of perks and assets such as property, investments and pensions. In Britain the top 10% own 5 times the total combined wealth of the bottom 50%, while in the US the top 10% own 10 times as much as the other 90% – and the top 1% alone own 40 times as much as the other 99%. As the joke goes, the top 10% own the United States of America. Which leads to that other joke about the American Dream – that you would have to be asleep to believe it.

What's this American Dream then?

It's not only American, as it happens, since there was talk in the UK about the British Promise and in France about the

Social Escalator. It was the assumption until about thirty years ago that with rising prosperity, if you worked normally hard, you could expect to be better off than your parents had been. Except that, with a few people at the top having more money that you or I would know what to do with, and with a million people at the bottom – many of them in work, believe it or not – reduced to using food banks run by charities, the dream has been shattered and the promise broken.

So what has happened over these thirty years?
A couple of things. For a start, we have seen the globalization of the economy. Of course, a more interconnected world economy has increased trade and has had positive effects – it has generally made for more peaceful relations and has, for example, lifted hundreds of millions of Chinese and others out of poverty. However, by forcing workers in advanced countries like the US or the UK to compete with low-wage economies in less developed countries, it has kept down wages while adding to the status and the income of those top executives now operating on an international rather than a merely national scale. This has been accompanied by a switch in investment patterns encouraged by too-big-to-fail banks, whereby the market became more like a casino, with hedge funds making money out of money rather than making money out of making things. And then of course you have the trickle-down theory.

So what on earth is the trickle-down theory?
It's just that, in this atmosphere, there was an ideological shift to a belief in a completely unfettered economy, freed of

government regulation of the banks, burdensome taxation or rules about working conditions. The idea was to let the market rip, to give everybody the chance to be a capitalist in a sense, so that more wealth would be created and, since this wealth would then trickle down to the less successful members of the society, there would be no need to prop them up with state benefits and allowances. The belief was that this would free everybody to become independent and to thrive in the great global marketplace of life. It was seen as liberating insofar as it would make people responsible for their own fate and encourage them to be strivers rather than work-shy skivers.

But the wealth didn't trickle down?
No, as we've seen, it gushed up to the top.

So whose fault was that?
Well, right-wing tabloid newspapers like the *Daily Mail* tended to blame the skivers, of course, suggesting that there were millions of people living off government handouts, occupying cheap council houses that often had spare rooms that they didn't need, and lying in bed in the morning behind closed curtains when the honest strivers were going to work. So the story was created that the welfare budget was inflated by all these scroungers and benefit cheats, giving rise to the myth that it was almost all being eaten up in this wasteful fashion.

A myth?
Yes, because most of the welfare budget actually goes on state pensions, towards which the recipients have of

course contributed, while the so-called scroungers – the unemployed and the sick – receive a very small proportion of the total expenditure. In fact, unemployment benefits account for just 4% of the welfare budget and cover all sorts of claimants, including middle-class people in between jobs. And in any case that is balanced out by those other benefits – which they don't even call benefits – that the same newspapers tend not to talk about.

So what benefits are those?
It's the whole range of tax breaks and incentives that are available only to the better off, from capital gains tax relief on a main residence to trusts for the benefit of heirs, offshore accounts and the whole galaxy of 'tax-efficient' investments conjured up by an army of tax accountants. Which of course emphasizes that salary differentials are only half of the picture, the other half being wealth, consisting not only of the ownership of houses, shares, pension holdings or second homes, but of the expectation of family legacies, the supportive network of valuable contacts, and so on. And the growing wealth gap is becoming more and more noticeable as the rich begin to live separate lives – increasingly in separate gated communities with private security guards as tends to happen in the United States – as though they were living in a separate world. Now I don't want to throw quotations at you…

I suspect you do want to throw quotations at me – to cheer me up even further!
Well just this one quote from President Kennedy, I promise!

For he did say in his inaugural address that if a free society cannot help the many who are poor, it won't be able to save the few who are rich. In other words, the rich and the poor are interdependent, and it is in the interests of both that there should be a fair balance. But the imbalance is increasing and having damaging effects in all sorts of areas, as well as on the economy itself. And I can see you're dying to ask me why.

Dying's a big word. But since you ask – why?
Increasing inequality is the effect not only of globalization, but of an economy dominated by banking, financial engineering, and short-termism in investment rather than by productive industry enjoying steady long-term support – an economy lurching along from crisis to crisis, from financial bubble to financial bubble. Inequality in its turn limits economic growth by restricting the amount that people can afford to pay for goods and services. It drives people into debt, creates wasteful bubbles with rising house prices, leads to anxiety and depression, and encourages crime. As various studies have demonstrated, more equal societies tend to be more prosperous as well as happier and more secure. So you'd better make the right choices.

You mean I'd be better off being better off?
It would certainly help, though you don't want to be so well off that you don't understand what's going on around you. If you were very rich, of course, you could attend one of the big public schools, where the fees would be roughly equivalent to the average wage, but you would already have enjoyed the essential advantages before you even got there. The awful fact is

that your destiny is basically determined by the age of five and, though there is great discussion of the pros and cons of different schools, no more than around fifteen percent of the variation in individuals' performance is accounted for by the quality of the school. It's all about whether you belong to a family that feels secure and in control of its own situation, whether it is a home where it is normal to read books and have reasoned discussion, whether you can have interesting holidays and structured out-of-school activities, whether you can assume that you could become a surgeon or lawyer like Uncle Jack or Aunt Jessica – in short, it's is basically all about *expectations*.

So how do I get those?
Well, it depends obviously on where you're born and when you're born. It's better to be born today than five hundred years ago and better to be in a developed area like Europe, where there is also less internal inequality than in South Africa or Brazil, say, because Europe has not yet let its market economy become a mere market society, where market forces control wages, health and education – in short, it's not entirely dependent on money. That's the good news.

And the bad news?
Oh, it's just that globalization has reduced global wealth inequality between nations but has increased inequality within nations.

But I'm still lucky to find myself here?
Yes, but let's not overdo it. There's still a lot of social inequality here in the UK – inheritance to begin with. If your

family owns stocks and shares, producing a nice unearned income, you're well away. Especially if they own a nice big house, steadily increasing in value since house prices have risen almost twice as fast as salaries over the past fifty years. Which means that both investments and house prices are doing most of the work for you before you even get around to finding a job or career and earning money for yourself.

So it's easier to be wealthy?
Well, middle-class at least. Especially since the tax system provides all sorts of allowances and tax dodges for the better off – who of course tend to be the ones who sit on committees and devise the tax advantages and are also the most likely to vote. It's a win-win situation.

But don't the others have houses?
Yes, 65% of people either own or are in process of buying a house through a loan they call a mortgage, but 62% of those that are owned outright are by oldies aged 65 or over, while only 1.5% of people under 34 own their house or flat outright. The rest have to slog away making monthly payments for around 30 years before they own it. And that's if you've been able to find the 10% deposit in the first place, which isn't easy since 50% of people have less than £100 in savings. So who can they turn to if they want to borrow money for the deposit?

The oldies?
That's right: the Bank of Mum and Dad, with almost half of houses and flats sold being bought with the help of parents or

grandparents. But that still means that the average age of first-time buyers is 35 and that 20% of young adults are still living with the parents. Housing is a big part of the way in which the system is still stacked against the young as well as the poor, even in a highly developed society. And of course, housing also affects the quality of education, as you can imagine.

Perhaps you'd better spell that out.
Well, it's not just that the wealthy send their children to the very private 'public schools', which not only have better staff-student ratios and libraries, but where they will form contacts with other wealthy kids that will serve them through life – quite apart from the fact that the 6% who are educated privately provide 55% of the students at the top Russell Group of universities. It's also that the standard of the state schools that everybody else attends is normally higher in the more expensive areas, so that if your middle-class parents can afford a house in the nicer part of town you're off to a better start.

So what does all this add up to?
To the fact that the UK has the 6th economy in the world, but only ranks 23rd for the quality of its primary schools.

Then what can middle-class middle children like you and me do about all this?
I didn't say I was middle-class, did I?

No, you didn't, did you?!
But it's a good question.

8. WEALTH AND CLASS

So what is the answer?

That it's not easy. When you're living in history and always in the middle of social and political change.

9. LIVING IN HISTORY
Social and political change

So living in history is living in time, isn't it? Even if the 300,000 odd years that modern humans have been around on the planet may not seem so long in the larger scheme of things – not, of course, that we know whether time is endless or not.

Do we need to?
God knows!

God again?
Sorry about that! Anyway, our humans have done quite well in the end, even if it took them around 200,000 years to spread outside Africa, move beyond hunting and gathering, and begin a more settled agricultural way of life. And it wasn't until around 4,000 BC that they had learnt to use the plough, make copper cups and bronze swords and, of course, invent the wheel – a very useful discovery, as you will readily agree.

9. LIVING IN HISTORY — Social and political change

Yes, that would have kept things turning around nicely.
But the next 4,000 years, up to the start of the Christian era, saw things speeding up with the development of writing and legal codes, a series of empires from China to Rome with great monuments such as the Pyramids, the Great Wall of China or Stonehenge – accompanied of course, by a series of wars.

Of course!
And since then, in the last 2,000 years, from a European perspective at least, change has become faster and faster since we have rushed through the fall of the Roman Empire, the growth of Christianity and Islam, the Black Death, the Slave trade, the Industrial Revolution, the French Revolution, the discovery of evolution and all the scientific and technological novelties we live with today – from the Internet or robots to nuclear weapons or artificial intelligence or that Euclid telescope that we've sent into space in an attempt to understand this mysterious dark matter that makes up most of our expanding universe. And I say nothing about the great rise in world population that goes along with it. Progress!

At breakneck speed, by the sound of it.
You could possibly say that. But of course, that's a distant view of human history, looking at it from a great height. In your own life you're only around for perhaps 80 rather than 300,000 years and you're working your way through the everyday relativity of your own situation.

So it depends when and where I'm living my 80-year snippet of the 300,000?

Yes, it's the luck of the draw. You're likely to have an easier and healthier life today than in the sixth century say. Some places are obviously more favourably placed as regards climate – California more so than Alaska or Italy more than Yemen or Sudan. You should be politically more comfortable in France or Sweden rather than in Iran or Afghanistan. And even at the local level, if you want a good school or a good job, you might do better in Brighton or Bristol than in Burnley, Blackpool or Bolkington-on-Sea.

Bolkington-on-Sea...?

Sorry, I get carried away by alliteration sometimes. Where were we?

The luck of the draw.

Ah yes. Because though progress appears unilinear and unstoppable when looked at from the global perspective, it is uneven at the local level. Not just because of climate variety, but because countries develop differently according to geography, agricultural or mineral wealth, belief systems and political structures. And if over several centuries Europe and North America enjoyed more progress than most regions in Asia, Africa and Latin America, it was because the industrial revolution and capitalism had developed in the West and because of colonisation, whereby western nations took valuable mineral and other resources from backward countries and developed them at home for rich profits.

9. LIVING IN HISTORY — Social and political change

Creating global inequality...
Especially since, in the earlier period, they operated a slave trade – forcing natives to work their own fields for a pittance or bringing them back for forced labour in Europe or America. Which meant not only more wealth for the West, but better health outcomes, more education and a better life for women.

But is that imbalance not being rectified?
It is to a degree, but there is still inequality across the world. Which is inevitable, with so many countries in the world – 195 the last time I looked – and at such different stages of development. Quite apart from the fact that they tend to define themselves as being different from – and of course superior to – the other 194 countries. On top of that, historical change involves so many factors – economic, social and cultural, not to mention the odd extra such as an earthquake or a pandemic – that the explanation is never simple. You remember Oscar Wilde?

The wallpaper man?
Yes, though he did also write the odd play. Anyway, in 1895, in the same year that he was imprisoned for two years for being gay, the feminist Edith Lanchester was put in a lunatic asylum for wanting to live with a man without being married – the poor woman was apparently suffering from 'over-education'. And as late as 1928, the writer Radcliffe Hall was seeing her Lesbian novel *The Well of Loneliness* officially destroyed, while the following year the Cambridge academic William Empson was sacked by his college after contraceptives were found in his rooms. But by 1967, when

homosexuality became legal, the contraceptive pill had come out and the public attitude to sex had become more liberal. So what had brought about this transformation?

You tell me.
Well, there had been all the social and cultural changes brought about by the Second World War, the widening of education and the increasing prosperity of the 1960s. Change is affected by all sorts of background factors and it's not a steady natural progression. Think of Kondratieff.

I'm trying to think of Kondratieff. But remind me, who is or was Kondratieff?
He was the economist in Soviet Russia who developed the idea that the economy moves in 50-year cycles. Which was fine until he made the mistake of saying that, even after declining in stages, a capitalist economy could recover.

So why was it a mistake?
Because they put him in prison for eight years and finally shot him. But then there was Schumpeter, who aspired to be not only the number one economist in the world but the best horseman in Austria and the greatest lover in all of Vienna. He argued that there were several cycles working simultaneously to drive the economy through innovation in a process he called creative destruction – constant cyclical change in fact.

And was he the greatest lover in Vienna?
I don't know, but that might be one reason why he skipped

9. LIVING IN HISTORY — Social and political change

off to America! Where he went on to argue that, even if there was progress overall, the economy was cyclical or dialectical, moving in waves just like the tide coming in and out. And since the economy is such an important feature of society, interacting with other factors governing war or peace, you can see how democratic progress also proceeds dialectically, advancing and retreating like the tides in a politically divided world. Just look at the broad movement of modern European history.

I'm looking.
In the 18th century, when books and newspapers were spreading, there was an optimistic Age of Reason in opposition to the age of royalty and religion. But after the French Revolution that was partly overtaken by the Romantic movement, which was concerned with the lonely individual rather than society and with emotion rather than reason.

From optimism to pessimism…
And then the optimism that went with the new technological progress – railways and all that – was accompanied by increasingly individualistic art and followed by World War One, which made a mockery of the progress until World Two made an even greater mockery of the progress and had people talking of the death of civilisation.

And is *it dying?*
Not yet. Indeed, there might just be another great pendulum swing of change on the way, since some are predicting –

if rather optimistically given the climate problem – that by 2050 not only will the global economy have doubled in size, but that six of the world's largest economies will be today's emerging economies. So the top five would in order be China, India, the US, Indonesia and Brazil, with the US dropping from 2nd to 3rd, Japan from 4th to 8th, Germany from 5th to 9th and the UK from 6th to 10th. A real turnaround.

Which would have political consequences?
Of course. For though with greater prosperity there's a greater sense, among educated people at least, that we are all living in the same world and facing common problems, you still have those 195 countries, each seeing itself as different. But it's not easy to be different in a world with a global economy where the decisions of the International Monetary Fund or the World Bank can matter more than local government decisions – leaving national sovereignty looking pretty hollow.

So...?
So they join a bloc for protection – the European Union, the Arab League, the G20 or whatever. But since they're still tied to collective decisions, there's often a lingering sense of loss of sovereignty and of national identity. Which can lead to a nostalgic right-wing nationalism and a return to the myth of the great leader – with autocrats like Russia's Putin or China's Xi Jinping beginning to be mirrored by Trump in the US and several European leaders in the West.

9. LIVING IN HISTORY — Social and political change

So it could all become politically rather messy? Any other complicating factors?
Well, religion inevitably…

So we talk about God at last? I rather thought you weren't too keen to…
Stop trying to be clever. Anyway, we need to talk about both religions and ideologies.

10. VALUES AND BELIEFS
Religions and ideologies

So to keep you happy, let's begin by talking about religions.

Religions in the plural? How many are there?
There were 4,200 or thereabouts the last time I looked. Big ones, little ones, old ones, new ones, some that believe in one God, some that believe in lots of gods – you name it!

So where do they all come from?
They came originally from an early time in human history when the first recognizably modern humans had emerged – as our old friend *Homo sapiens* – from millions of years of evolution and were trying to understand what the hell was going on. It's hard today to imagine the situation of these early hunter-gatherers as they tried to survive in a dangerous world where unknown others or strange animals could be lurking behind every bush – where everything living on land or sea seemed to survive by killing and eating everything else. They didn't know where they were or why they were.

10. VALUES AND BELIEFS — Religions and ideologies

They didn't know why that big shining ball slid from the sky every evening, or whether it was a different one that rose on the other side of the sky the next morning. They didn't know why the skies got angry with thunder, why there were droughts or floods and seasons that came and went, why some among them fell sick, died and slowly crumbled away. Indeed, they weren't always too sure about where babies came from.

No?
When an unknown jungle tribe was discovered not too long ago, it turned out that the natives thought birth had something to do with the phases of the moon – which is not as silly as all that, when you think about it. Those early people were after all doing their best to establish their place in this mysterious world. But they didn't know that the earth was round or that it circled around the sun – it was a good hundred thousand years later after all, in 1633 AD, that Galileo was condemned to permanent house arrest by the Pope for suggesting such an absurd and iniquitous notion.

Yes, it might have seemed a bit counter intuitive.
Nor did they know our solar system was part of a Milky Way galaxy containing hundreds of billions of stars and at least as many planets. Or that the observable universe contains at least two trillion galaxies.

A proper galaxy of galaxies!
So how could they know that the earth was around 4.5 billion years old? It was as late as 1654, after all, that the

scholarly Archbishop Ussher was publishing his finding, based on scrupulous examination of Biblical texts, that God had created the world on the 22nd of October 4,004 BC – at 6p.m. to be precise.

Just in time for dinner!
And of course, evolution only came along in the mid-19th century with Darwin.

Who suffered ulcers, migraines, dyspepsia, flatulence and a few other horrors in consequence, if I remember.
You're being frivolous. We have to understand the situation of those early people, wandering around for about 100,000 years in small, isolated foraging bands in a world of mystery and menace. Imagining divine or demonic forces to be driving the forces governing their lives, whether sun, fire, storm, thunder, wind, love or war.

Primitive polytheism?
Exactly. And indeed the first significant developed religion to appear was Hinduism, which developed on the Indian sub-continent and would be followed eventually by other polytheistic versions such as Jainism, Sikhism, Buddhism and, inevitably, hundreds of local variants in different areas. However, the situation on the ground had been changing since the invention of agriculture around 11,000 years ago, which had led people gradually to a more settled existence in larger tribal communities. Which of course brought the problem of keeping the increasingly larger group together, of developing a system of shared values, aspirations and

loyalty to a leader which would protect them against rival tribes and other dangers. A structure which would provide a template for understanding the larger, universal mystery confronting them and would lead gradually...

You mean they began to create God in their own image? Instead of God creating man, man creates God?
It was inevitable, I suppose. And with the invention of writing increasing the pace of change, it was in the Middle East that the dominant monotheistic strain developed, starting with Judaism around 1,400BC, followed by Christianity – which of course gave its name to the present era – and then by Islam, founded by Muhammed in 622AD. And since Christianity and Islam are the two largest religions in the world, you can see the problem.

You mean because monotheisms are by their nature absolutist – 'my God is the only true God, so your God can only be a fraud'?
Yes, and since absolutism breeds intolerance and violence, they have always been opposed to each other – Christian Crusades and Muslim Jihads. Each is also divided internally, with conflict between Catholic and Protestants on one side and between Sunni and Shia on the other – amplified though the derivative sects on each side. And each depends on God revealing himself through an individual human – Jesus or Muhammed.

So how are you supposed to view religion today?
Well, it's a little complicated. It's true that, while Christianity and Islam did make contributions to our knowledge in the

past, our modern scientific world view has little place for religion and that, as Christhopher Hitchens put it, theology has given way to philosophy, astrology to astronomy, and alchemy to chemistry. Our perspective today is based rather on what we do not yet know about a vast expanding universe than on a global doctrine derived from one small planet at a pre-scientific time. And both Christianity and Islam are open to too many other criticisms.

Such as?
Well, it's not just that both the Bible and the Koran were put together long after the events described and that they inevitably contain inconsistencies and contradictions. It is also naive to believe that religion is the source of morality, which derives rather from social interaction, mutual sympathy and understanding. Especially in view of the historical association of both of these religions with violence.

Both externally and internally, you said...?
Yes. Both presented themselves no doubt sincerely as religions of peace, but if you absolutise difference and see real or possible enemies as evil, you are inevitably drawn into violence and holy wars. After all, in Deuteronomy God tells his chosen people that they must show no mercy to those He has defeated in order to provide a home for them, but destroy them totally, while for many centuries the Christian church accepted slavery, torture, burnings, and full-scale wars. At least, we've had a separation of church and state in the Christian world since the 18th century, so that people are no longer being oppressed on grounds of religion.

But that's not so in the Islamic world?
There has been some movement in that direction. If Iran, Pakistan and Afghanistan are full Islamic states, others have merely incorporated parts of Islamic law into their constitution. But Islamic opinion is still intolerant of individuals who abandon the faith and there has been a series of terrorist attacks in the West, not to mention Iran's Ayatollah Khomeini issuing a decree and offering a large reward for the assassination of the novelist Salman Rushdie – who was attacked and badly wounded in New York.

Shouldn't you perhaps also mention the basic problem of defining God?
You mean the old Arian controversy? God, the Son and the Holy Spirit are said to be all one, but if God begat the Son how could they be equal? I'm more interested in the fact that the Church of England has lately been trying to decide whether God should be described in these gender-conscious times as a 'he' or a 'she' or possibly a 'they'. Because women haven't done too well out of religion.

Since they're 'defective and misbegotten', as you reminded us, according to Saint Thomas Aquinas?
Well, it's understandable that in the earliest times primitive men were mystified and therefore repelled by the reality of menstrual bleeding and birth, which conferred upon women a certain otherness and fed the notion – which lingers on in Judaism – that they were 'unclean'. Also, the threat of sex to the social cohesion of the group in difficult times called for firm control, but the blame was transferred neatly from

men to women – it was Eve who ate the apple, it was the woman who incited the man's desire, who threatened the peace. Christianity dealt with the problem by sublimation, by having Christ born of a virgin, but women tended to be legitimised only as mothers or virgins, there was the cult of celibacy in the Catholic church, and none of this helped the advancement of women.

And what about Islam?
Islam sees itself as protective of women, which in practice means keeping them under the control of men, closely tied to the husband's family and free from the danger of contact with male outsiders. The situation varies with the level of modernization, but in Iran a revolt of young women against the compulsory head covering was recently harshly put down. In Afghanistan, of course, they are treated like children, unable to move around unaccompanied and protected from being tainted by education. But that's going against the trend.

You mean religion is dying out?
Not so much dying out as changing. The majority of people in the world are still formally classified as having a religion, but that's partly because the belief overlaps with nationalism and ideology. It is difficult today for the educated Christian to believe in heaven with choirs of angels and hell with horned devils, or for the Muslim to accept President Erdogan's assertion that the recent devastating earthquake in Turkey which killed 59,000 people was part of Allah's plan for humanity. So the believers are being forced to see all this as symbolical and poetic.

10. VALUES AND BELIEFS   Religions and ideologies

'Forced', you say…?'
Don't underestimate how painful this transition away from religion has proved to be, whether at the personal or the collective level. Religion has for so long clothed people's lives from cradle to grave with ceremony – baptism, circumcision, confirmation, marriage – that it has not been easy to abandon. It has meant family, community, the nation, the continuity of a rich cultural tradition and the comfortable sense of living safely within a system in tune with the cosmos. It's one thing for religion to be reduced to tradition for the educated in advanced countries, but for so many people in the world at large…

Yes, I can see why it's not so easy to talk about religion.
Even so, the action since the Enlightenment in the 18th century has shifted towards ways of looking at the world that are based on reason and science rather than on miracles and stories of revelation. In fact, the Age of Religion has become an age of ideologies. And the fellow who invented the term and started the switch was a French philosopher called Destutt de Tracy, who had plenty of time to work out his new 'science of ideas' when he was sitting in the Conciergerie prison waiting for Robespierre to order his head to be cut off during the Terror in the French Revolution.

And was his head cut off?
No, it was Robespierre's own head that was cut off. So de Tracy could get on with developing this new social science designed to transform France into a rational and humane society by combining individual freedom with state planning. Napoleon was very taken with all this initially, but once

| 101

in power and obliged to make political trade-offs – even though he was an agnostic, he found it useful to make certain concessions to the Church – he started to see the ideologues as airy-fairy theoreticians not living in the real world. And almost immediately the term ideology came to be seen in both a positive and a negative light. As you'd expect, of course.

Why would I expect?
Well, the 19th century was the great period of industrialization and revolutions which would eventually lead to the First World War. So you had the new sociology of Auguste Comte living alongside the class-based analysis of Karl Marx and then the whole field of social analysis splintering into the communism, fascism and nationalism that would lead to the Second World War. You then had the Cold War and the nuclear threat, after which you had the innocent hope that the development of global trade, the consumer society, the mixed economy and a degree of global culture might bring about a convergence of world views and the end of conflict.

But it hasn't brought about that convergence?
Not yet at least, but let's be optimistic. And meanwhile, since we're living in the world as it is…

We should talk about relationships…
You took the words out of my mouth.

From where else?

11. RELATIONSHIPS

Social and romantic

So even in the more complex society of today people tend to live in manageable groups as defined by occupation, class, educational background and so on. And it's obviously more comfortable if you have the same political or religious views, speak with the same accent, read the same newspaper, watch the same TV channel and at least pretend to follow the same soccer team.

Peer pressure.
Yes, but you should at least try to recognise the board you're playing on and try to avoid groupthink. Even with the vast amount of information available today – or perhaps because there's so much available – so many people seem to live in silos, get impatient with complexities and follow posturing populist showmen rather than political programmes. The structures we live in – and indeed the language that goes with them – are limiting. They're probably more in control of us than we are of them.

You're saying it's not easy to be an individual?
Yes, you can be yourself so long as you're more or less like everybody else. This was the problem that was so much discussed at the time of the Enlightenment in the 18th century – except that the very form of the upper-class gatherings in which they discussed it merely exemplified the problem.

This was at the famous salons *in Paris?*
Yes. For they began to see conversation – even when discussing serious philosophical questions – as a public performance, almost as an art form. That they were meeting in the elegant setting of an aristocratic drawing room, with ladies present, had something to do with dictating the tone, of course, but to be successful in this situation was challenging. You had to dress stylishly but not extravagantly and remain gracious even when the subject threw up real political or religious differences. You had to speak eloquently but not too eloquently, be serious but not too serious, be witty but not sarcastic, be amusing but not tell jokes and, in short, be perfect but not tiresomely perfect.

Unwritten rules…
But they didn't remain unwritten for long, for there soon appeared a torrent of behavioural and conversational guides designed to tailor you for success in public.

Even so, it all sounds a bit too frilly French, doesn't it?
It's true that the 18th Century English upper class didn't indulge in such refined conversation, if only because the

sexes were segregated after dinner and the ladies retired to discuss embroidery or whatnot, while the men remained to smoke and swear and spit into the fire and talk about farming. Which merely encouraged the authors of guides to behaviour in polite society to continue their civilising work – in English this time.

Which suggests that the individual's relationship to society at large…
Is problematic. If not as problematic as his or her relationship to another individual when it comes to falling, as we say – not rising, but falling – in love. And I hardly know where to start.

At the beginning?
OK, so we belong to a species and people need people just as monkeys need other monkeys – a prime cause of death for both being loneliness. And of course any species has to maintain itself as best it can, doesn't it? Which it normally does by the females suckling their young and by members of the herd combining to try to fight off attacks from prowling predators – wolves or hungry lions. But as we've already seen, humans are exceptional since their young are so helpless after birth and take so long to learn to walk and become independent…

The price to be paid for their superior brainpower and adaptability…?
Exactly. So you need something specially tailored to the situation, some force of attraction and enchantment that

will bind a couple together and, even if the magic changes gradually over time into contentment and peace, produce a stable relationship suitable for bringing up children. And that's love, romantic love. Old Plato may have thought it was a serious mental disease, but it's essential for the survival of the human species.

And do we know exactly how it works?
Well, we needn't go too closely into the brain chemistry involved – the role of oxytocin, pheromones and all that – or explain why the lovestruck Napoleon found Josephine even more desirable when she hadn't washed. But it's true that despite the famous song in that old film *Casablanca*, a kiss is *not* just a kiss.

So what is it?
It's an intimate exchange of scents, tastes, textures and emotions, as the neuroscientist Judith Horstman pointed out. Which triggers a cascade of neural messages and chemicals that transmit tactile sensations, sexual excitement, a sense of closeness and even euphoria. It's telling you basically whether you are genetically compatible and whether the chemistry is right. Not of course that you would be perceiving it in such laboratory language. You would be wondering in more romantic terms whether this other person is desirable and possibly even special to the point of being 'the One'.

The 'One'?
Yes, the 'other half', as some call it. Sex is not just fun or a

release from nervous tension. Even at its most basic level it is a way of achieving togetherness with another human being and by extension with the whole human family. But when it's experienced romantically as love, it transcends gender difference, satisfies an underlying need for wholeness, takes you beyond desire, relates you to the universal and offers an escape from mortality… What's the matter?

Are you OK?
What do you mean: 'am I OK'?

Well, you know: 'offers an escape from mortality'? That's not possible.
Quite. That's the point.

You're talking the language of religion.
Because human love and religion have interacted throughout civilization almost to the point of fusion. You get erotic imagery in the Song of Solomon in the Bible, or the ecstatic vision of Saint Theresa of an angel penetrating her entrails with his fiery golden spear and leaving her body on fire when he withdraws it. If the sacred and the profane are often conflated, it is because the desire for completeness engages the same part of the brain, as another neuroscientist Semi Zeki points out. Which makes for a certain amount of confusion in the traditional and almost mystical depiction of love, which for all its tragic grandeur, is basically about…

Impossibility?
Yes. Firstly, because the romantic dream of a love that is

timeless and transcends the relativity of life is not compatible with a world where you are subject to accident, ageing and death. And secondly, because it is not compatible with the need of a society to maintain its coherence by means of rules. And the tragic hero or heroine, or both together, tend to be those who infringe or rebel against the rules. Think of Romeo and Juliet, who are both driven to choose death…

Or Isolde, drinking poison with her lips locked to the dead Tristan, in one last kiss…

Or Tolstoy's aristocratic Anna Karenina, who abandons her husband and son for a young bachelor and is finally driven by isolation and guilt to throw herself in front of a locomotive. Or Cathy in *Wuthering Heights*, or Flaubert's Madame Bovary – the list goes on. And these are the rebellious heroes and heroines that conventional audiences secretly identified with before reverting to their orderly conventional lives. Freedom and danger by proxy.

But hasn't the situation been changing over the past hundred years or so?

Yes, romantic love is more tied to a time when religion played a greater part in people's lives and when the norms of society rendered sex outside marriage immoral. The drive is still there of course, the attraction of a shapely female form or a deep male voice, as well as the need to escape loneliness and the pain of rejection. But the board you're playing on has changed considerably since the Second World War.

11. RELATIONSHIPS — Social and romantic

Though you're talking basically about the more individualist Western world, aren't you?
Yes, but with the spread of modern communications the picture is changing – even strictly Islamic Iran has difficulty dictating what women wear on their heads. The world in which we're living has got larger and freer, if more complex. People may still tend to look for partners of a similar social and income level, but we're a long way from the tightly class-structured society of seventy or eighty years ago. When your choice of partner was limited, when before the Pill came in sex was limited and clumsy even for engaged couples, when the wife was generally less qualified than her husband and would give up her job on marriage…

Leaving her financially dependent on the husband. Quite different from the two-salaried couples of the situation today…
When the nature of work is changing and more women than men get a university education so that society is more mobile and there is more room for experiment, when the balance between the couple has altered and young men can be seen pushing prams in parks while their wives – or partners, since they often feel no obligation to be married – catch up on work or whatever. Quite a change.

And very much for the better.
Certainly, there's more room for freedom and self-realisation when you're operating in a more open society which is less constrained by formal boundaries, custom and inflexible moral codes. But then freedom doesn't quite come free, does it? You've got to work at a relationship to keep it alive

through all the changes and stresses that life can throw at you.

And that's assuming that you find the right partner in the first place. From your phone, of course!
Yes, we're living today in a world of social media where a teenager can have a thousand contacts and no friends. And where the world of dating, with its endless possibilities, can be both bewildering and stressful. We've now got around 1,500 dating sites in the UK, some free and some paying, catering for everything from casual one-night stands to serious relationships for 20-year-olds, the over-50s, graduates, rural dwellers, Christians, Jews, Muslims and every category you could think of. And ironically, since of course people can get quite nervous about how to behave to their advantage with someone new on a first date…

It brings us back to the problem of self-presentation of those social climbers in the aristocratic salons of 18th century France.
And here too help is at hand. If you're nervous you can try alcohol, but don't overdo it. To ensure that you're sending out stronger and more captivating vibes you can prime yourself with that oxytocin nasal spray you can buy online, though you perhaps shouldn't overdo that either.

And if that still doesn't reveal the real you and render you irresistible…?
Well, there are professional instructors in dating, who organise weekend or even weekly courses designed to bolster your confidence, improve your self-presentation, and run

11. RELATIONSHIPS — Social and romantic

you through rehearsals of the dating encounter until you can hopefully take it in your stride. They're not cheap, of course, but you may feel it's worth the investment.

So long as you don't fall for the instructor, who's only professionally pretending! It's all so complicated these days, isn't it, and sometimes so punishing for people. You almost wonder if it's worth it.
But it *is* worth it. In the freer and more equal society of today, it may make life more complicated, but it's also more realistic and generally more rewarding. You agree?

Of course I agree. It's not as though I had much option!
I suppose that's true!

You do realise that it's yourself you've been talking to all this time?
Yes, but I've nobody else to talk to. And at least this way I get a higher quality of conversation with an intelligent sparring partner.

Thank you very much!
You're welcome!

---

12. FACING THE FUTURE
Climate change and its consequences

Would you like me to start?

Be my guest.
OK, so there's only this one hot subject these days, isn't there? Apart from earthquakes in Turkey, Morocco and Libya, we are now seeing wildfires breaking out across the world from Portugal and Greece to California and British Columbia and of course floods cropping up from Austria and Sweden to India, China and Doha. We've seen millions displaced, homes devastated, public property destroyed, crops ruined and deaths ranging from hundreds in Hawaii to 140,000 in Myanmar. In short…

…we've got a climate crisis. And it's more than just a climate issue.
So where do we begin? Land, sea or air?

Land sounds pretty basic.
Then let's start in Egypt, which has been called the cradle

of civilization, after all. With an organised society on either side of the Nile going back 6,000 years, which of course has left us the great pyramids and the Pharaohs' tombs. You remember flying upriver that time from Cairo to Luxor and then on to the Aswan Dam beyond? When you looked down, what did you see?

I saw the river shining below. Flowing between green cultivated land on each side…
And beyond that, on each side…?

There was only a sort of brownish desert. Not a bit like your soft seaside sand – just brown, rocky, arid, inhospitable desert.
And what does that tell you?

That we may be made of starstuff, as your friend Carl Sagan said, but we're dependent on water for our existence?
Exactly, that we're a by-product of water. And, as it happens, the Nile is an interesting example. It's the longest river in Africa at around 4,000 miles, but the rain falls mostly beyond its southern border, so 85% of Egypt's water has to come from the Nile – and it may be further reduced by that new dam upriver in Ethiopia. Which means that water from the river – usually processed over and over again – has to sustain life for over 100 million Egyptians. But it can only do it at a cost.

Though since we all use water for absolutely everything – drinking, domestic uses, drainage, watering fields, watering animals, drilling for oil or coal, and industrial activities of all

| 113

kinds – we hardly notice the inevitable result. Which is that the land is sinking.

Exactly, and that's the first dimension of the climate problem. The delta of the Nile is a broadly triangular basin about 100 miles north to south which meets the Mediterranean in a white sweep 155 miles wide between Alexandria and Port Said. Its rich silty soil is the most fertile in Africa, but since it slopes gently downwards by 52 feet before meeting a rising sea, it is facing loss of land, soil damage through salination and the threat that it could see 700 square miles of land flooded, with up to 5 million people displaced by the end of the century. And that's just one illustration of a larger problem.

Which is of course that around two-thirds of the world's population live within 100 miles of the sea and that the majority of the world's largest cities are in coastal areas threatened by rising sea levels. So Jakarta, the capital of Indonesia and a megacity of over 10 million people, is sinking in places by around 10 inches annually. Mumbai in India, with a population of 21 million, is seeing its infrastructure increasingly damaged by heavy flooding...

Or take Japan where Kobe, which had already sustained serious damage and over 6,000 deaths from that big earthquake, has suffered heavy flood damage, as also has Osaka where the cost has been estimated to be some 200 billion dollars. And that's without even mentioning the two largest economic and political actors in all this, the United States and China.

And yet we've had climate deniers who claim that there's nothing new about all this, that there have always been natural changes

12. FACING THE FUTURE Climate change and its consequences

due to variations in the earth's orbit or tectonic changes in the earth's crust and, moreover, that greenhouse gases such as carbon dioxide and methane are necessary for keeping the earth warm enough to sustain human life. Which sounds plausible until you learn that last year was the hottest year ever.

The fact is that since the Industrial Revolution we have been pumping more and more greenhouse gases into the air so that, instead of keeping the earth at a stable temperature, we've been heating the planet at a much faster rate. Since 1900 the level of carbon dioxide has risen by 40% and indeed there's now more of it in the atmosphere than for the past two million years.

So how exactly did we get here? Apart from the fact that that we've been planting crops more and more intensively for thousands of years, and increasingly using nitrogen for fertilising, which can release nitrous oxide which is 300 times more damaging than carbon dioxide.

And we've been rearing animals which – since they have frankly no sense of decorum – fart out methane, which is 30 times more powerful than carbon dioxide! Don't mention it to the first farmer you meet, but a single cow can emit up to 100 kilograms of methane per year.

I'll try to avoid farmers – and cows. Anyway, along with agriculture we should mention deforestation, the cutting down of forests for industrial purposes or to make way for more intensive agriculture. Especially since trees not only perform the valuable function of capturing carbon dioxide from the atmosphere but release the stored carbon damagingly when they're burnt.

But of course the real villain of the piece is the burning of fossil fuels such as coal, gas and oil, which contain carbon dioxide that had been safely buried in the ground for thousands of years until we started mining operations. Once we started burning fossil fuels, we were releasing the stored carbon dioxide into the air.

So what about the effects of all this on people?
Well, they're obviously not good. Melting polar ice leads to the sea level rising around the world and the damaging effects on coastal cities that we were talking about, while the melting of mountain and sea glaciers raises the temperature. Rising temperatures cause heatwaves, droughts and wildfires, which not only destroy villages and threaten humans, but kill off indigenous animals – like the three billion affected by the Australian wildfires of 2020. Drought and less fresh water mean it's harder to grow food, obviously, while extreme temperatures and polluted air are damaging to human health. And of course, with the oceans warming and the sea becoming more acidic, the coral is dying and the fish are struggling to adapt – just like the insects, plants and animals.

And the humans by the sound of it! How did you all – how did we all – allow things to get so bad?
But like so many others you're not taking account of the central dimension of the climate crisis, though it's the one that nobody seems to notice.

You mean the population increase?
Exactly. At the start of the Christian era the global

12. FACING THE FUTURE Climate change and its consequences

population of around 200 million was a tiny fraction of what it is today – it was a different world. It took until 1800 for it to reach 1 billion, but since then its rise has been exponential, doubling to 2 billion by 1928 and soaring to 8 billion today – in fact, it has risen fourfold in my lifetime. What does that tell you?

Apart from telling me that you're not as young as you were, it tells me that all the change in the world since 1800 has been due to the Industrial Revolution.

And to the improvement in every area which subsequent technological progress and globalization have brought about. Look at the availability of information through the web and television, or the transformation in communications across the planet – you may take a call in a jungle these days. Look at the advances in science and discoveries in medicine, leading to a longer lifespan, better living conditions and better health. Look at the effect of the globalization of women's football for that matter. The hard fact is that, viewed in perspective, the thirty odd years since 1990, when globalization really took off, have seen more improvement in living conditions than the previous 3,000. It has been a triumph.

And potentially a catastrophe.

Well, it's the old paradox that the good and the bad tend to go together in this world. Also, it's unfortunate that the crisis should come at a point when the world is so obviously still divided between the advanced and the undeveloped halves. But 195 countries, rich and poor alike, did sign that

United Nations agreement to try to limit global warming to 1.5 degrees above pre-industrial levels by 2030.

And what have they been doing about it – even the countries with serious problems that you mentioned?
But it's costly and politically difficult. And there's a long-term choice between, on the one hand, taking the drastic steps required to *prevent* the damage inflicted by flooding as currently predicted and, on the other hand, trying progressively to take just enough defensive steps to *accommodate* to the change. So Egypt has built a wall of concrete blocks 22 miles long on the beach to protect Alexandria and is creating a new administrative capital away from Cairo – though that may also be politically convenient. Indonesia is also moving its capital Jakarta to an island a thousand miles away, as well as building a protective seawall.

But what about your largest two 'economic and political actors', the United States and China?
Well of course China is the world's chief emitter of greenhouse gases and it certainly has problems with its coastal cities. Tianjin has seen the sea rise by almost 4 inches a year, while Shanghai – with its name, ironically, meaning 'on the sea' – should see much of its surface submerged by 2050. But the Chinese have been taking a gamble by maintaining a longer reliance on coal in the interest of political and economic stability.

So it's all about limiting *the damage as best you can, rather than preventing it? And does that go for the US?*
So far yes. New Orleans, which of course saw serious flooding

12. FACING THE FUTURE Climate change and its consequences

in that deadly hurricane Katrina, plans to reduce flood hazards, raise existing buildings and create a new sustainable environment. New York itself, where the sea level is said to be 20 inches higher than it was in 1860 and which is at risk with so many tunnels and bridges in the city, is planning to protect the business area and is building a seawall on Staten Island. Though its overall approach, like that of Miami, has not exactly been…

Convincing…?
Well, it was hardly sensible to talk about measures against flooding while subsidizing the building of luxurious high-rise apartments in derelict waterfront industrial zones in New York or on the seafront in Miami. And in Miami there is also the particular problem that it stands on a bed of highly porous limestone, which acts almost as a sponge, so that protective walls and seals on buildings are unlikely to give adequate protection if the sea goes on rising freely. Which you'll tell me raises the question asked by Naomi Klein and others as to whether the economic system which created the problem is likely to be able to solve it.

And that COP 28 summit presided over in Dubai by the boss of the United Arab Republic's state oil company provides you with the answer. We'll only limit global warming to the necessary 1.5 degrees centigrade by 2030 if we get rid of oil and gas, and we're already behind schedule, but there was no plan, no time-table, only vague talk about 'transitioning' away from oil and gas and an attempt to divert attention to carbon capture and storage, which we all know would be both inadequate and hopelessly expensive. Let the wildfires rage, let the crops die from drought, let Samoa and Fiji sink into the sea, just so long as the fossil fuel billionaires flourish. COP 28 was a right royal cop-out.

All very eloquent, but we've got the economic system we've got and it was in a way logical to have an oil state as the venue. It situates the problem where it belongs and the continuing floods and fires and droughts will hopefully keep the pressure on. The irony of course is that, as the World Economic Forum has concluded, a properly controlled transition to net zero – which there would be just about time to achieve – would benefit the world economy by over 40 trillion dollars over the next few decades, while a top European study says that it could lift 3 or 4 billion people out of poverty. As investment flows reverse direction and follow the money, the problem would eventually be solved. It's just that the need for speedy implementation is obvious. And that there's a glaring conflict between the global good and the perceived self-interest of almost 200 separate countries, each with its specific problems, in a world divided between developed and underdeveloped, rich and poor.

Because the political crisis may be global, but people's interests go on being local and national – look at the territorial conflicts going on across the planet, or the Gaza nightmare or Putin's imperialistic nonsense in Ukraine, not to mention the growth of populist politics in the West. Indeed, the very seriousness of the climate threat can deter people from thinking about it, especially if they're old enough to believe it can never really affect them. It's looking pretty hopeless.

I wouldn't say that quite yet. Difficult things in this world

12. FACING THE FUTURE Climate change and its consequences

tend to get done only at the last minute when there's damned well no alternative and as the situation worsens the pressure for change can only increase. Pressure at global level, pressure on governments within countries, pressure on the oil companies whether in Saudi Arabia and China or the US, Britain and France, pressure from rising migration. I'm not saying we'll solve it in good time, or solve it completely, or that we'll be the saviours of Samoa or Fiji, but we have the technological means to solve it and we'll probably scramble some sort of solution as we usually do. We'll do it the hard way, but we'll do it.

'You're a bit of an old optimist, aren't you?
It's the only useful approach.

13. FACING THE FUTURE
AI and darker matters

Would you like to start this time?

That's gracious of you – though I suppose it might just be my turn. Where were we?
We were getting on to artificial intelligence, or AI as we call it – which just shows how familiar it has become.

Yes, it has been creeping up on us for the past 50 years or more and now, often without realising, we're using it every day. We can ask our black ball Siri to light up and tell us how far it is to Exeter or to play a favourite piece by Mozart, and we've now got our own co-pilot on the computer which can tap into a whole range of search engines. We've got generative systems that can recommend films or purchases based on user ratings, game playing systems that can make a chess champion look like a beginner and creative systems that can turn out a university essay on Hegelianism, a typical novel by Dickens or Dostoevsky, or a 'lost' painting by Poussin or Picasso – not to mention ChatGPT,

13. FACING THE FUTURE   AI and darker matters

which can produce realistic conversations about this, that or the other thing. It can be a little eerie sometimes – you never quite know whether you're talking to a person or a ghost in a machine.

Yes, it can be strange when you bother to think about it, or when you find so many iPhone addicts blundering blindly into you as you walk along the street. But then AI is just so useful in lots of ways, isn't it? Your 'ghost in the machine' is your smart assistant like Google Assistant or Cortana that can answer queries, make suggestions and perform various tasks. AI can skim through and synthesize documents at lightning speed, which makes it invaluable in a whole range of areas such as business, law or medicine. And it's not just that it saves time, since in many cases it's doing work that in practice wouldn't get done – because it would take too long or cost too much.

Ah yes, cost. Which is of course what drives the rapid introduction of robots in manufacturing, assembling, packaging, transporting and so on, with only the occasional human straying on to the shop floor. And AI will obviously have an increasing role to play in long-term transport, though I'm not convinced there will be a great rush – even if they were affordable – to buy a self-driving car. Driving is one of the few practical skills left for people – men perhaps in particular – to practise these days and they mightn't be keen to have it taken away from them. Along with so much else.

You mean the loss of jobs?

Yes. And not just for professional drivers, but for travel agents, librarians, cashiers, administrative assistants – anybody

handling data, dealing directly with the public or playing an intermediate role in management. And that's not even mentioning the creative and cultural side – actors, composers, musicians, novelists and so on. You saw those strikes in Hollywood, didn't you? People are beginning to feel threatened.
Which is understandable of course, but isn't that's just the way humanity progresses, in painful jolts? Look at the upheaval in mindset caused by the invention of printing or the discoveries of Galileo. Look at the silk weavers of Lyon in 1831, sabotaging the new machines threatening their jobs with their wooden clogs called *sabots*. Or look at the miners, striking to protect their dangerous and unhealthy way of life in the face of mechanization. Improvement comes the hard way and the losses you mentioned will probably be replaced by new and possibly better jobs in medical research, graphic design, cybersecurity and areas we haven't yet thought of. Perhaps it's just that change appears to be so much more rapid than before.

But it's also so much more radical than before. Chess players actually like playing chess and are proud of their skill, just as car owners often fancy themselves as drivers – yet suddenly these things seem old-fashioned and diminished. Writing a novel or painting a picture seems less of an accomplishment if you're competing with mountains of artificial artefacts manufactured by AI. Are we being bypassed or sidelined by our own creation?
I suppose it depends on how you view AI. You might see it simply as a useful tool, which just happens to be thousands or maybe millions of times faster at playing chess or synthesizing and collating documents than humans are, so

that it's both labour-saving and cost-saving in a whole range of areas. But of course you can still ask questions about who is using it and for what purpose. Some specialists in the field of AI, such as Kate Crawford, see it as being the latest expression of the fusion of capital and political power.

Well there are certainly concerns that the surveillance and data collection techniques used by the state intelligence services are being blithely copied in such areas of activity as the screening of air passengers, of people attending political meetings and even of ordinary citizens in the street. Which of course merely reflects the now pervasive techniques used in business and commerce – checking identities and credit worthiness, evaluating the performance of workers in factories, facial recognition of customers in banks and supermarkets, identifying potential customers through their reading habits, medical issues or food preferences, feeding them more items to purchase and so on. It's a system that creates its own shadow in the form of scamming. And with Google on top of all that there's nowhere to hide any more.

Are you perhaps exaggerating a little bit? Isn't it just another case of the good and the bad, the positive and the negative, going together and needing to be managed? Look at what AI can do in the field of medicine and healthcare, for example, not only by improving medication, diagnosing illnesses earlier and performing surgery, but by providing care and comfort in old age – making life better and longer in fact. Look at how it could transform education and health in the developing countries. Look at the wheeled robots or the drones delivering shopping or your evening meal to your door. Or indeed look at the ways in which it could be used to help the climate crisis itself, by facilitating smarter energy saving systems or more efficient renewables. Look at the gain.

And look at the cost. We're losing our privacy and moving into an interconnected world by using not just social media or the internet but all sorts of other devices – anti-burglar devices, smartwatches, smart running machines and who knows what else? My phone is recording my heartbeat, my blood pressure, the number of steps I take in the day, and so on. With the aid of AI, companies like Amazon or Google can collect all this information, create a commercial equivalent of us, tempt us with potential purchases, feed us ideas, influence us, guide us, condition us, and pretty much control us. We're already on the way to losing our identity – and possibly the sense of our own humanity – if we're living with robots.

But the robots are already here and many of them are enhancing our lives in a variety of ways, not just by taking over repetitive tasks in offices and on assembly lines, but in education, for example, by personalizing teaching or supporting students with learning difficulties. And look at what they can do for the elderly and infirm, not only doing the vacuum cleaning and other household tasks but acting as friend and companion.

Yes, but we seem to be moving into a world where you could grow up with a robot assistant – called John or Joanna as you fancied – who could serve as babysitter, tutor or friend as required and where, since both information and entertainment are becoming increasingly personalized and immersive, you might be distancing

13. FACING THE FUTURE — AI and darker matters

yourself from other people. Though if you find yourself lonely and lacking in friends you can always get yourself a robot lover – ravishing female or handsome male called Gianni or Giannina as you fancy – who will see to your emotional needs and sexual fantasies in expert fashion. Are we turning ourselves into cyborgs, part human and part machine?

Well, we've already been moving a bit in that direction, I suppose, with our pacemakers, artificial limbs, implants, defibrillators, hearing aids and chatbots telling us at what age we're going to die and whatnot. And nobody is complaining about that.

But so far we've only really been talking about the weaker forms of AI, whereas they're moving towards so-called super AI systems which could not only perform any intellectual task better than humans but might even uncover parts of reality beyond our understanding. Where on earth would that leave us?

Well, there are leading scientists like the late James Lovelock, who think that there's no problem at all, that our integration to whatever extent with robots is a wonderful and perhaps inevitable new stage in the development of the human species, bigger than all the progressive turning points that went before. We've only been around on the planet for 300,000 years after all and it's a mere 400 since Galileo told us the sun moved round the earth and only 150 – no more than a couple of lifetimes, after all – since Darwin told us about evolution. Could the optimists be right?

Or could they be disastrously wrong? Could these new hyper-intelligent beings be beyond our control? Could they really discover areas of reality totally different from ours and beyond our understanding? Or simply destroy our civilization and us along with it?

Well, the idea that robots could discover a kind of reality totally different from ours seems a little far-fetched, since it would be limited to the terms of our presentation of our own reality. And why *would* they destroy us all? They would be as dependent on the health of the planet as we are, and therefore as dependent on organic life as we are, so I think the romantic idea of evil robots taking over the universe, or of vengeful cybernetic androids looking like Arnold Schwarzenegger is best left to late-night movies. On the contrary, we're likely to find AI very helpful in dealing with the climate crisis. Meanwhile, we need to try to get agreement across the planet on the avoidance of the misuse of this new tool.

Which doesn't look so easy. Especially with rising migration adding to the wars in Ukraine and the Middle East, and the rise of semi-fascism in the West. We've already seen autonomous hunter-killer drones being used on both sides in Ukraine and they are designing others which can fly much longer distances while avoiding detection. And that's only a hint of what might be to come. What other clever new weapons will be coming out of those rising military budgets?

I wouldn't fantasize too much about some final grand self-destructive global war. We've had nuclear weapons for nearly 80 years and the mutual fear of immediate reprisal has kept the peace quite effectively – a balance of terror, if you like – so if it came to it, I'd expect the same sensible fear to operate again. In any case there are efforts going on throughout the world to maintain control of AI. Especially since we don't want to see any use of fake news or images in the political domain, for example.

Especially since we've already seen damaging fake news in US politics. Especially since many specialists think that AI-generated fakes could become undetectable. And especially since you've already got 'bad actors' all over the place, with authoritarian governments controlling the narrative and interfering in democratic elections, media that largely serve special interests and criminal gangs annexing people's identities so that we're moving towards living in a splintered world where you can't really trust anybody or anything.

But you're wandering again into the dystopian fantasy of the *Brave New World* of Aldous Huxley – the million million spermatozoa man, you remember? – or of George Orwell's *Nineteen Eighty-Four*, with its Ministry of Truth.

Except that we already have in Communist China a society practising the most sophisticated forms of thought control as well as political control over its citizens.

I know, but you can't create a mature society while infantilizing your population and China, as it develops further, will be driven beyond that contradiction. And it has to recognise like the rest of us that the world now seems to be at a pivotal turning point. This climate crisis is a life-or-death challenge to humanity, but to the extent that it deals with it – however messily or belatedly – it can only gain in strength and unity. And the potential increase in capacity that could come from AI could dramatically transform our grasp of our situation in the universe.

Here we go again! The old optimist in full flight...!
Because the climate problem is only part of the significant turning point we are living through at the moment. You realise that no human who has ever lived has had the faintest idea of where we are or what we're supposed to be doing on this little ball rolling along with other balls around that shiny bigger ball in the middle of nowhere?

Yes, the thought has occurred to me that we might be rather marginal.
Well, with the Hubble telescope and now the James Webb Euclid telescope – you've seen those wonderful close-ups of a faraway dying star or of that group of galaxies colliding – we're beginning to get some answers, or at least some indication of the extent of the problem. You know of course that the universe is now thought to be composed of 68% dark energy, 27% dark matter and only 5% normal matter – the visible bit that we belong to.

I also know that we are simply inferring dark matter from the gravitational pull that something or other is exerting on visible matter, just as we are assuming the existence of dark energy from the fact that something seems to be operating against gravity to push galaxies apart and make the universe expand. Which means that we don't understand 95% of the problem.
But the Webb telescope has years of discovery left and then there will be more telescopes and more discoveries. The

13. FACING THE FUTURE — AI and darker matters

universe is about 14 billion years old and we've only been around for a sliver of that time. Yet we're the only living beings even able to ask these questions as far as we know…

Precisely! As far as we know…
But it could well be helpful to discover life on other planets. It might lead our warring tribes here on earth to realise that we're all in it together and stop fighting irrelevant battles. So we should be optimistic and see ourselves as being only at the beginning.

Well, except…
Except what…?

It's going to take a long time.
So?

You don't have very much time. Which means that I don't either.

———————————

14. LIVING IN TIME
Lifespan, ageing and death

So where did we end up last time?

We were talking about time itself – as I suspect you remember.
Well time is relative, isn't it? It depends of course on where you are in the universe and in our little solar system the length of a year for each planet depends on its distance from the sun and how fast it's orbiting around it. So the equivalent of our year on earth would be around 165 years on Neptune…

… but only about 3 months on Mercury.
And even psychologically time is relative. Remember those endless summers you had as a child, yet as you age you can't believe how quickly the summer disappears and the years spin around faster and faster You were in your prime the day before yesterday – it's all just so relative.

But there's nothing relative about the calendar. It's absolute – year upon year upon year up to old age and death.

I know, I know. But you've got to be philosophical about it.

Some of the philosophers were a bit too philosophical about it! Socrates was condemned to death in Athens for mocking the gods and forced to drink hemlock. Seneca got on the wrong side of Nero, had to cut his wrists open and bleed to death in a warm bath. Giordano Bruno didn't quite agree with the Inquisition and was burnt to death. Thomas More was beheaded by Henry the Eighth for not being enthusiastic about Henry's shift away from the Catholic church. And that's not even to mention those philosophers who philosophized directly about cheating death by prolonging life.

Like Francis Bacon and the chicken?

Yes, he was travelling through the snow on Highgate Hill one cold winter's day when he had this bright idea. So he bought a chicken from an old peasant woman, killed it, gutted it and filled it full of snow to freeze it and see what happened.

And what happened was that he caught a terrible cold and died, as I remember.

Yes, but I was thinking more of Descartes, who liked to work all day in his nice warm bed and dreamt of living for a thousand years so that he could complete his philosophical system. But then he was flattered into travelling to Stockholm to teach philosophy to Queen Christina, except that it was wintertime and she liked to see him at five o'clock in the morning when her mind was free of royal business. So he too caught a terrible cold and died of pneumonia – at the not so impressive age of 53.

So much for philosophy! Then let's see what religion has to say on the subject of death, especially since it's in fact the central problem for religion: what to say about death? You remember when that very tall, dignified Indian guide led us down to 'holy Ganges', as he called it, to see the Hindu death rituals at the sacred city of Varanasi?

I'll never forget it. A vast stretch of stone steps leading down to the river, three or four funeral pyres burning smokily, chanting groups carrying bamboo stretchers with corpses covered in flowers, bells being shaken, a queue of people way up on the left waiting to have their fortunes read by wise men sitting at desks, cows scrambling and slithering on the excrement on the steps, men bathing or standing waist-deep and praying in the sewage-polluted river and, above it all, the monkeys – silhouetted against the early morning sky as they danced along the tops of the buildings and ran around everywhere as though they were in charge of this carnival of creation. To think that families from far away should spend their savings on putting ailing family members up in local hospices so that they could die and be cremated in Varnasi!

Yes, but it wasn't just death tourism. Hindus believe in the permanence of the soul, which on death is then recycled into some other body, and the family members were hoping to break this cycle of reincarnation. Buddhism, of course, is a little different.

Yes, Buddhists don't believe in a permanent transferable soul, but rather in mental energy or consciousness, which is released on death and dispersed into other life forms. So in Tibet corpses could be cut up and placed on the mountainside to be eaten by vultures, while in the Philippines they could be hung on the faces of cliffs or in caves. The body is simply being given back to nature.

Christianity, of course, has death at its very core, doesn't it? You only have to see the Crucifixion scene in the stained glass of a Christian church or survey the stone crosses in an old graveyard to see how fundamental to the Biblical story it is.

And it's a starker story. So according to the dominant version God creates Adam, creates Eve from one of Adam's ribs and leaves them naked, innocent and free in the Garden of Eden, while just telling them not to eat of a certain Tree of Knowledge. But this serpent tempts Eve, who tempts Adam, who eats the apple, and by committing this original sin they lose their innocence. And since 'the wages of sin is death', they not only condemn themselves to be mortal but they hand down death to all of humanity. For 'as sin came into the world through one man and death through sin, so death spread to all men'.

But then Jesus comes along, born of a virgin and the Holy Spirit, founds the Church and dies by crucifixion, with his death being seen as atonement for humanity's sin. He is then raised by God from the dead and ascends unto Heaven, from where he will return one day in the Second Coming to judge the living and the dead. He is therefore seen as a member of a Holy Trinity of Father, Son and Holy Ghost and, in effect, as the presence of God on earth.

You'll tell me, of course, that this was a fable appropriate to these early times, so it's hardly appropriate to ask the obvious

factual questions – such as why didn't God know in advance that Adam, whom he had created, was going to eat the apple?
Yes, but fable or not, it bound together in one story the mystery of death, a creation story and the issues of morality and love.

That may be so, but it created problems for the Church itself. There was the old trinitarian-versus-unitarian dispute. There was the problem of what should happen to all those who died before the Second Coming and the Last Judgment – which led to the Catholic Church having to invent the indeterminate waiting period of Purgatory. And of course there was the big split at the Reformation, followed by the intellectual challenge from the Enlightenment and modern science, which has led to the decline of Christianity in the West and a proliferation of variants right down to the God-and-guns evangelicals in the US. But it no longer has a role in social or political control, and nobody today is dreading a Hell of 'weeping and wailing and gnashing of teeth', with little grinning devils prodding you with their tridents for all eternity. We've enough problems as it is.

Yes, we did agree that religion in the West had been demoted gradually into being seen rather as a tradition or even an aspect of national culture. So there was no mention of Hell when the churches mourned the supreme sacrifice of soldiers after the First World War – whether on our side or the German side. And of course, the sidelining of religion has tended rather to sideline death itself, hasn't it? In Victorian and Edwardian times, death was a permanent shadow over family life since you tended to die earlier and die at home,

14. LIVING IN TIME — Lifespan, ageing and death

and family life was correspondingly more austere, with praying before meals and children told to be seen and not heard. But with improvements in medicine, life expectancy in the West has risen from 45 years in 1900 to around 80 years today. And in this more secular society death has lost its terror and its grandeur.

Certainly, things today are very different. Kids no longer listen dutifully to their grandad but help him out with his iPhone. Wives have jobs and a more equal status, while teenagers have their own noisy and impenetrable sub-culture. And the retirees, members of the new Third Age, are spending their 'golden years' doing Pilates, working out in the gym, jogging, playing tennis and swanning off on trips to Benidorm or Lanzarote or cruises to the Arctic and the Mediterranean.

And in between times they're pursuing free courses of all kinds with this University of the Third Age invented by the French, playing Sudoku and Scrabble and taking whatever steps are necessary to remain mentally, physically and sexually active into their Seventies and Eighties. It's a great life if you can stand the pace.

Yes, but it's 'use it or lose it', as they say. For death is still there, isn't it — on the horizon, waiting for you? And the question now is whether with all our modern science there's anything anybody can do about it. There are plenty of places studying ageing, aren't there? Like the Immortality Institute in Houston or those in Phoenix and San Bernadino in the US, or the Oxford Future of Humanity Institute and other university institutes in the UK. Not that there's anything new about all this, since the discovery of evolution had led to all sorts of people taking an interest in questions about the length of life and heredity.

And not that any of the early ones got very far. Élie Metchnikoff, the 'father of gerontology', thought you could live until you were 150 if you stopped smoking and drinking and damaging your insides with the wrong food, so he recommended Bulgarian yoghourt and consumed more and more Bulgarian yoghurt until he died of heart failure in Paris in 1916 at the age of 71. Serge Voronoff, known as the 'monkey gland man', saw the answer in transplanting fresh genital glands into men, but since young human donors were reluctant to come forward for some reason, he had to resort to chimpanzees – the results were less than persuasive and he died after a fall at 85 in 1951. Then there was Alexis Carrel, whose view that society should be run by an aristocracy of superior beings and that criminals and the criminally insane should be eliminated was much appreciated by the Nazis. It's as though there was a certain nostalgia even in science for the idea of immortality.

Because it was written into the culture through the old religious mythologies. Within the Christian story alone, you have Methuselah living for around 969 years. Noah for 950 and Adam for 930 years – although Moses is only said to have lived for 120 years. But since then, you've had people having serious doubts about what life would be like if the dream of immortality ever came true. In Swift's Gulliver's Travels, Gulliver *comes upon a group of immortals called the Struldbrugs, who hate every mortal minute of being immortal, while Mary Shelley in* The Mortal Immortals *saw it as an absolute nightmare and indeed Aldous Huxley – why does that guy keep cropping up everywhere? – poked fun at the dream of prolonging life indefinitely in his 1939 novel* After Many a Summer Dies the Swan.

That's not to say of course that, with all its resources, modern medical science won't be able to lengthen life to some degree. As it happens, the oldest verified lifespan that we have to date is that of the French woman Jeanne Calment who was 122 years old, though deaf and almost blind, when she died in Arles in 1997. Which is some way from immortality, but it fits in with the view of some specialists in the field that we could achieve a general lifespan of 120 years and perhaps move experimentally towards 150.

Which would mean that you could have a child of 120, a grandchild of 90, a great-grandchild of 60 and a great-great grandchild of 30 – all multiplying similarly in their turn – until you increased the population even further and dislocated the whole society. Doesn't sound like a great idea!

No, but in opposition to all that the anatomist Leonard Hayflick and others suggest that we're not designed to play around with our lifespan, that our usefulness in the evolutionary process lies in our ability to produce healthy offspring, which is why the menopause acts as a cut-off point for women and men gradually lose their sexual mojo – which would still leave Viagra as a lifestyle choice, I suppose.

Of course there are those, mainly in the US which has an annual Frozen Dead Guy Festival in Colorado, who think you can outwit the evolutionary process with cryonics. So you get frozen immediately on death and hung upside down in liquid nitrogen for perhaps 500 or 1000 years, when medical science will hopefully be able to cure whatever you died of in the first place. It began in the late 1960s and it has so far been performed on at least 500 people, mostly men. It is highly expensive, especially if you want your pet dog or dormouse to be frozen as well, but not quite as expensive to have only the head frozen, to be connected eventually to a robot – though Jeffrey Epstein apparently wanted both head and penis to be revived so that he could spread his DNA more widely through the population. So what's not to like about cryonics?

Well, it literally is a deadly gamble, isn't it? For if the scientists know how to freeze you, they don't yet know how to unfreeze you successfully after your 500 years or whatever. In any case, there is no guarantee that the cryonics company involved would even exist by that time – several have already gone bust. And you only have to imagine somebody from the Middle Ages waking up in today's world of air travel, global communications and nuclear fusion to visualise the nightmare of arriving in a similarly altered world without family, friends, connections or relevant cultural assumptions. They could put you in a museum.

So you're saying then, aren't you, that there's no escaping death? We can't see it religiously or romantically as the portal to some higher world, or as the moment of revelation of some transcendent truth. So we try to forget about it in our 'golden years' by jogging, playing Sudoku, following courses and going on trips to Lanzarote or wherever.

But we're not doing these things just to forget about death, we're doing it because we enjoy them. This is often the most carefree period of our existence. It's part of life!

Yes, but then things begin to go wrong. You lose your partner. You fall and break your pelvis or a hip, lose your mobility and fail to get it back, or you're diagnosed as having some disease you have never heard of. You become dependent on crutches, then on a wheelchair, you are not able to join in normal social activities, your family gets you a carer and then goes on to install you in a care home. Old age, as Mae West once declared, 'is not for sissies'.

But it's not always as bad as that and in fact care homes can be comforting and sociable places. So what are you suggesting?

Wouldn't you be tempted to keep control and die on your own terms? You don't have to step under a bus or jump off a cliff these days if your condition is incurable, you can go to Switzerland if you can get there and can afford it. Euthanasia under strict medical supervision is also practised in the Netherlands and in Belgium, where you can pass away peacefully surrounded by your relatives. There's growing interest in it here as well.

Yes, but doctors are supposed to cure you rather than kill you. Euthanasia is still open to abuse by relatives for financial reasons unfortunately, also you mightn't want to legalise it in case somebody wants to go back to the days of Alexis Carrel and the Nazis. In any case, medicine is so advanced these days that in the vast majority of cases dying can be relatively painless. And if you're terminally ill and unable to respond, the doctors may quietly consult your relatives about whether to withdraw life support in order to save you from suffering. *Yes, but our secular funerals tend to be so damned efficient and businesslike these days, don't they? With the crematorium turning over bodies every half hour and the car park already beginning to fill up the for the next customer. It's so functional, so unromantic.*

But it doesn't have to be. And I find it preferable to treat a funeral as a celebration of the life of a friend or family member, rather than as a ceremonial farewell to wave him or her off for eternity to a blissful eternal Heaven or a horrendous eternal Hell that neither would believe in. You remember where we started, with the 'million million spermatozoa, all of them alive, out of that cataclysm but one poor Noah dare hope to survive'?

'But the One was me'?

Exactly. You see how privileged you are to be here in the first place – in the only part of the universe where we know that life exists? Privileged again to have found yourself in a developed part of the planet? And privileged even beyond that to be alive at the very moment – the real challenging crunch point – when civilization is threatened by climate change as by the sophisticated weaponry we've devised to annihilate one another…

A privilege indeed!

… and, above all, when with our Hubble and Webb telescopes and other ventures into space we might begin for the first time to get some real idea of the scope and nature of this cosmos that we play our tiny and fleeting part in. I wouldn't care to miss it.

You were accusing me of being romantic. You're the romantic! But a romantic realist, I would hope.

After studying at Trinity College Dublin
and the École Normale Supérieure
de Paris, Cecil Jenkins taught at the
universities of Exeter and Sussex, where he also served
as Dean of European Studies.

His writings on France include books on The Nobel Prize-winning novelist François Mauriac and the novelist and art historian André Malraux, as well as A Brief History of France and A Brief History of Paris.

He has also published two novels,
including a prize-winning crime novel, and had three
stage plays performed - one in New York – as well as
two plays on Radio 3.